*Divan of Ghalib*

# Divan of Ghalib

Nachoem M. Wijnberg

Translated by David Colmer

WHITE PINE PRESS / BUFFALO, NEW YORK

White Pine Press
P.O. Box 236
Buffalo, New York 14201
www.whitepine.org

Publication of this book was made possible, in part, by grants from
the National Endowment for the Arts, which believes that a great
nation deserves great art; the Dutch Foundation for Literature, and
with public funds from the New York State Council on the Arts, a
State Agency.

Cover Design: Elaine LaMattina

First Edition

ISBN: 978-1-935210-85-6

Printed and bound in the United States of America.

Library of Congress Control Number: 2015943684

# CONTENTS

# Foreword

Nachoem Wijnberg is an acclaimed, prolific and ambitious twenty-first century poet who writes in Dutch and lives in Amsterdam. Mirza Asadullah Beg Khan, best known by his pen name, or *takhalus*, Ghalib, was an acclaimed, prolific and ambitious early-to-mid-ninteenth century poet who wrote in Urdu and Persian and lived in Delhi. Both poets are known for their sovereign appropriation of poetic traditions, appointing themselves as the legitimate successors and chief interlocutors of the great poets of the past.

Ghalib wrote much of his work in the classic form of the ghazal. One of the most striking characteristics of many ghazals is the way they conclude with the poet addressing himself with his pen name. This allows the poet to start a dialogue with "the poet." In the hands of a master like Ghalib, this can be an immensely powerful technique. In this book, celebrated in the Netherlands as his masterpiece, Wijnberg adds another level by writing ghazals that link Ghalib's traditions and knowledge with his own, fearlessly drawing on everything to consider everything.

Like any decent *divan* (which simply means collection), it opens with the creation of the world, then goes on to the rest.

This *Divan of Ghalib* is not a book of translations of Ghalib's poems. It is not even a book of poems loosely inspired by those of Ghalib. It is a book of English translations of the Dutch poems Nachoem Wijnberg wrote for Ghalib and with Ghalib, with Ghalib and to Ghalib.

*The Divan of Ghalib*

## The Beginning

What is it again, what is discussed as if it's a solution,
    Made in the workshop of light and dark, like the beginning?

How far up do I need to go to see the earth, all of it, and some sky
around it?
    Like seeing all of something that happens, just far enough to
see the beginning and the end and a little bit around it.

Why don't you give that to me as a gift, the difference between profit
and loss,
    So I don't need to say why I am starting here and not somewhere
else?

Afraid of starting on something I can't do without a lot of help,
because I am not good at it and give up easily.
    It began and stopped, just when I wanted it to go on until the
beginning was enough for me.

The beginner and the quitter, does one of them get better as they
grow older?
    Suddenly one has time for the other.

Do I want to know that? No, I don't and should have said so sooner.
    Look, I had no idea how much I was giving up, but now you
are going to show me.

I want to start again, and you've already started,
    So I don't want it to count.

I've heard that others start well, but I don't.
    That's why it is so difficult for me to say I want to start.

Do I want us to start again at the beginning, so I can be at the beginning?

Are you offering to start at the beginning, so I can be at the beginning?

I notice that, without saying anything, we have started again at the beginning,

It's not that I saw the beginning last time, but a great deal is being clarified in large steps, like at the beginning.

I have to do the last bit alone, I've saved something for the last bit.

Someone else was at the beginning, but I didn't see him.

Waking among flowers and getting paid for it, being able to skip a day if I feel like it.

No one brought me here, I can still turn around and walk in the other direction.

Music to run by, right through the Sinai Desert, past Mount Sinai.

Did I see someone standing still in the middle of the desert, as if on the beach around Mount Sinai?

The end having something to do with the beginning, that's unusual, it is only like that here.

The rules I am able to obey provide beginning and end, that's why I can start later than I expect, tell me it's so.

## Ghalib

Ghalib lives in a house in Delhi,
    But when he's writing poems, in the middle of Iran.

No one reads Persian anymore, not even in Iran,
    And Ghalib says the Persian dictionaries they sell in Delhi are
full of mistakes.

The pearls from the king of Persia's crown, one by one I drop
them on the page.
    The king of Delhi's crown, which I have transformed into poems.

Removed in plain view, given to me in secret.
    I know that paradise does not exist, but still I think of it often.

The door of paradise is just like your door, though less busy.
    What is a crown, a thing to put on your head, what does it
crown, it crowns what you think.

Ghalib writes such dazzling poems,
    He deserves a stipend, but today he doesn't know who to ask.

## If the King Pays Me

If the king pays me, I will write about his garden as evening falls,
    Like a woman beckoning him with a finger or a group of blind
dancing girls, a gift from far away.

He shows the dancing girls where they will live the rest of their lives,
    Which doors lead to their rooms and which doors are wardrobes
in which they can hang their clothes.

My mouth full of jewels or my weight in gold,
    I would be happy with either, no idea which is worth more.

God summons an angel and has him bow down before Adam,
    Is he king for a day, says the angel, oh right, I can already see
his bride walking toward him.

My wife is drunk, she thinks I am magnificent and my breath is
sweet.
    This is how I would like to be paid, with more than my weight
in life.

Who else should they make king, there's nobody else left?
    When I am king I won't need to be afraid of them putting
someone else in my place because there is nobody else left.

If God is like a king over all he sees, but surer of his throne,
    Why isn't he more generous to a poet like Ghalib?

## Ghalib and One More

At court they still act like it's the old days,
    But instead of long parades with horses and elephants, the same
horse keeps coming past.

It's the best they can do with what is left,
    Like the consolation of being held, the smell on the clothes.

There is enough wine to keep filling the same glass and passing it
round,
    Reciting poems all night long.

I say I'm going to wash my hands, then stay away a couple of hours.
    When the night is almost over I come back and they ask me for
one more poem.

After that I am the first to go outside,
    Catching sight of the woman who stands on the street till
morning comes.

It is she who will receive me in paradise,
    When no one she looks at desires her any longer, she recites
poems by Ghalib.

## Ghalib and the Angel

I am standing in the street waiting for an angel, I don't know
which direction he will be coming from.
    Who would ask me how the world is made, if not an angel?

On the last day of each week man is made,
    That's why an angel has a body like a man's, after that there is
nothing else.

Must I wait for the angel that comes to ask questions of the dead
in their graves?
    He carries a shovel because the dead are buried deep in the
ground.

The angel comes running up to me while I am still letting my eyes
get used to the light.
    He hadn't heard that it's the day the dead will be set free again.

Playing a game of chance with an angel, who do you think will
win?
    If I sold umbrellas it would never rain again, not a drop.

A ship in a storm and I am the only passenger, who do you think
they will throw overboard?
    The angel asks if I would like to play another round, my luck
is sure to turn.

Ghalib died yesterday, I stand up and sit down again.
    As far as I'm concerned, he can die again tonight, after
a hundred times I'll have a better idea how much I care.

## There's Not Much I Need to Know

If I talk about Jamshid, I only need to know that he was king of
Persia,
    That he could see the whole world in his wine glass.

If I talk about Sikandar, it's Alexander who took Darius's kingdom,
    And spoke to Darius's wives as if each of them had been
married to him her entire life.

More than just drinking from the glass in which he could see the
whole world, Jamshid invented it,
    Just as Sikandar was the inventor of the mirror he hung as far
away as possible.

Khidr cannot die because he cannot afford to pay his debts.
    No one gives him a pittance—for a king it's a pittance—so he
can pay his debts.

Khidr can no longer die, not even if love consumes him from
within.
    He promised to tell Sikandar where the water was, but sent him
in the wrong direction.

What it's like to have someone who can no longer die travel
beside you for a while:
    He says he knows the way, but also talks so much on the road.

The reason I stay with you is because you spoke with the one I
think about every day, the one who died.
    Ghalib is talking about what suddenly comes closer when a
friend tells you about it.

## Ghalib and God

God looks at us one at a time to decide if he would like to marry
one of us,
   That means it's the last day it will be possible.

God is thinking of someone who resembles him, the way a man
resembles him,
   A bird with a face on both sides of its head, and decides not to
make it.

If I think about myself and my desires, I sometimes think it was
like that with me too,
   That it was worth spending a morning thinking about how to
make me, and that was enough.

I raise a hand to my mouth as if holding a glass,
   To show how much I once drank before leaving the house.

Who has taught me to be so generous?
   If the previous glass was the last, you will still give me another
if I say I am going.

A night full of stars, Ghalib lifts it up in the morning
   If he has slept all night, not needing to go anywhere.

## Advantage

What is the advantage in knowing how something ends,
    Being able to ask someone who wants to explain it to be quiet?

I can't find something and I have looked everywhere I thought it
might be.
    Shall I look somewhere else first or look again where I have
already been?

It's too difficult to find my way from place to place to see if I can
see what I am trying to find.
    Maybe someone else can take me from place to place?

I've heard that nothing has ever happened that wasn't good for me
too.
    Silence, muted light on grass, there must be an advantage for
me in that.

I've told everyone I won't be here this evening,
    But I haven't gone far because I kept coming back to make sure
no one was at my door.

That might not be the place with the best chance of finding me,
    But if someone is looking for me there and I am not there, that
someone will be lost.

I sell the wine Ghalib drinks when evening has come.
    As payment I take what Ghalib has when evening comes.

## Ghalib and the Angel of Death

When I am lying naked with my eyes shut it is because I am no
longer afraid.
    That only counts if someone is lying next to you, says the
angel of death.

When the angel of death comes to me, I ask permission to finish
what I am doing.
    Even if he says that this time he wants to kiss me and can't
promise how he will do it later.

I offer to work for him while I am at it.
    The angel says, you know what you'll do if you've done it a
day, you'll show how easy it is.

The angel of death has light wings, weighing almost nothing, the
wind can blow them away.
    Try lifting one up.

You, with those two wings in your hands,
    The night is almost over and you can come and lie next to me
until morning has come.

Ghalib why do you talk so much about the angel of death, as if
you have known him for such a long time?
    You should see him again soon, otherwise he'll think you don't
feel the same way about him anymore.

## By Heart

I think about something as if I will lose it if I tell myself I will
never have it again,
    And I recall being someone who never said anything for no
reason.

In the past I couldn't keep up a conversation with someone in my
head if I didn't know where that someone was.
    Now I can keep it up as long as I like, maybe I could have done
it then too, I just didn't dare.

I want to write down everything you have said and learn it by
heart,
    So I can read what I know by heart if I want to.

Here comes yet another person who says that if he could write for
the first time,
    He would start with what is easiest for him to learn by heart.

In the daytime God speaks to Moses.
    At night he leaves him alone so he can learn what he has heard
by heart.

Learning things by heart, but not by repeating them over and over,
the way I used to learn things by heart.
    It is like the first day out of prison, everything is so big.

## Write Down What I Owe You

I thought it was free but they asked me to pay,
  Which I would have agreed to. I mean, if it had been offered
to me beforehand, I would have said yes and not asked for more.

I need help to stay between full-out and dead on my feet.
  Having to finish my drink is my excuse for not getting up.

I pretend to write something on the palm of one hand with a
finger of the other,
  That's how I ask for the bill without having to speak.

Turning upside-down tables and chairs the right way round so I
can choose a table,
  That's a job for angels and waiters.

My body is made of clay, that's why I can write on the palms of
my hands.
  If I hold my hands up in the air for a day I can no longer
change what is written there.

This is how I learned to write: someone wrote a sentence and I
wrote a sentence under it in a different color.
  It was easier if we pretended to be negotiating something, for
instance, a price.

Who will sell me something that is only like a dream, Ghalib?
  I want to lie in bed with a storm outside and keep waking up
to a memory of the dream I have bought.

## More and More Freedom

If you can decide whether or not to do something there must be
something that allows you to see a difference.
    That is not possible if you are alone at the beginning.

A decision is the same as moving or staying in the same place,
    But seen from two different points.

I didn't come up with these clear arguments,
    They were a gift from someone who remained calm and polite.

I would like to put the second to the test, and have come up with
a clever plan to do so:
    Slightly moving one of the two points.

There are so many points, but you and I only know a few, maybe
only those two.
    I would give all my clothes to be alone with you one more time.

You only make one exception to not thinking that something is
true because you want it to be:
    Being more free when you want to hold tight to someone who
can't hold tight to anything, Ghalib knows what that's like.

## Ghalib and Mir

Mir says that God plays chess like a beginner who takes every piece he can.
   It's easy to beat him if you can play against him.

The one who made the world, but not me.
   When he forgot to make someone else there was always something to remind him, but nothing reminded him of me.

I have decided to look for a different job, even if that means throwing away everything I have learned.
   I have decided to write in a language no one speaks anymore, there's no one I can ask for help if I don't know a word.

What increases when which chance becomes smaller?
   If I have increased my vocabulary by writing down every new word I hear?

I think I do have an idea of what makes a good experiment, but can only explain it in a language I do not yet speak,
   Which I hope to learn without effort when I am not doing anything else.

I have stopped writing the history of the world.
   I wasn't very far along, it's not the kind of thing you do without an advance.

Instead I am writing a diary, in Persian as if it were spoken like that in the beginning.
   I would rather make up a new word than use one that comes from another language.

I write poems in the language I speak because almost no poems have been written in it.

Today I would like to be someone who can say he doesn't want to do anything in the next ten years except learn languages that have been around a long time.

It doesn't matter which language I write in, as long as I more or less get what I'm asking for,

As long as I more or less arrive where I wanted to go when I asked directions in the street.

Ghalib, you're not the only one who can write,

They tell you that long ago there was also someone called Mir.

Mir, so they say, walked down the street in the middle of the night and could go no further.

It could also have remained quiet while he walked back and forth between two corners of a room.

## Ghalib and Hafiz

The Persian poets are silent and Ghalib comes in shouting,
  Telling them his poems are on the way, look, here they are.

The rules Persian obeys and the way Persian turns its face to
someone,
  They are inside of him, as deep as possible.

Adam's garden is a small garden, a few paces long and a few paces
wide.
  That's the garden Hafiz stands in when it has turned dark and
he wants to go somewhere.

I have tied myself to a tree to stop me from steering the garden
toward you like a ship
  When I hear your voice somewhere.

Had I thought the garden was empty, that there were no more
animals wandering around it?
  These are the animals that can call each other by name, only
their children were sent off after Adam.

If the garden were to be divided up I wouldn't be able to continue
to wait in it, not even in my part,
  Because it would only be a part on paper.

Go ahead and say which part you would like, you can go first, we
don't need to take it to court.
  Long after we've divided everything up, I can come back and
say, you don't know who I am, but I used to hide in your garden.

I help your children to write their poems.

    Afterwards they can fold the paper to make burning ships and explain to you how they've done it.

In a room in Hafiz's house a ship is waiting
    For the day land and water will be reunited.

Ghalib has a ship like that too, a friend's children made it for him.
    Not for such a big day, but for a very small one.

## A Plan

I always carry out the same plan.
   I could have known beforehand that I would lose what I love
the most if the thing I could not allow did not happen.

The one who took it from me wakes with a start from a dream
and gives it back to me,
   And more too, for the time it was his, although he hasn't
touched it.

As they have never seen an elephant, they run away when I pull off
the cloth that is covering it.
   If that had failed, I had another plan and another, because only
having one plan is like going on a journey with an elephant.

If an elephant doesn't want to continue in a particular direction, it
kneels down in that direction,
   Like the elephant that dreams of India and, still dreaming,
starts to run there.

I want to send something ahead to the person who has
experienced everything I can imagine.
   Before he leaves, I want to tell him everything I know.

I ask someone else to wait where I can call him,
   So that I can send him after the one who has already left if I
remember something else.

If desire keeps me awake at night, I send an invitation to someone
who has had that same desire for longer,
   Then I can see in advance if there is any point to what I can
still learn.

It has again reached the stage where I have to go in search of
someone to talk to,
    Opposite each other, then beside each other, near the water.

Ghalib, I need someone who sounds like you, it's reached that
stage, as if I can't help it,
    Having to search for someone again, as if that's still possible

## Question and Answer, How We Do It

Ghalib has been dead a hundred years, you see that immediately,
   But I still remember how quick he was, one question after the
other.

If Ghalib could choose whether he'd wanted to be a man or a
woman,
   He would say you only needed to wrap an arm around him.

Please appear unexpectedly at my door once again,
   I won't pretend to be surprised.

It takes me a long time to remember
   When you said we would be staying together forever anyway.

It was mid-evening, mid-summer,
   Just before it began to slowly grow dark.

We had spoken to each other and I had gone outside,
   And you followed me out and then we went for a walk together.

I long for you because you are the only one who can tell me I am
mistaken, I still have something left.
   I am not startled when you tell me I can take a moment to
reconsider my answer.

We have hardly noticed that Ghalib is dead.
   He was already so tired, even if he pretended not to be.

I want to know as much as possible about the earlier lovers.
   They are not even alike, Ghalib, are you going to try to be more
like this one or that one?

## Too Much, This Much

What do you want—me to tell you I don't know much about you?
    You're right, an eye and a throat, that's about all.

The hours I couldn't sleep, not out of longing for someone,
    But because I was scared of what is not enough.

I am too old to join a procession, even if it's just the two of us.
    One is the beginning and one is the end, I keep having to stop and stand still.

The bird up in the sky, what use to it are feathers, what use to it are wings, where can it hand them in?
    At the rose that can't bear this much evening, Ghalib lays them down next to it, on the dark earth.

## In the Desert

That's a job that would suit me, building a wall straight through the desert.
  Not to keep anyone out, but as the last remaining wall of a house.

I stand before Mount Sinai,
  Afraid as if I can see someone with pockets full of money, who says I can borrow some from him.

He stands there lending money to those who have nowhere else to go.
  You're right, Ghalib, if he were really alone no one could see him.

When I had just left Egypt and didn't know what to do next,
  I was given part of the law in advance, the rules for the day I must not make anything.

Those who were not children when they left Egypt grow old in the desert.
  They walk back to Egypt after embracing their children one after the other.

# Fire

Something that keeps going so I can return to it, it doesn't keep
going forever, it's actually soon over,
  But I can't keep wandering around in a deserted place for that
long either.

This is for those who have heard that I cannot get by without it.
  A fire burns faraway, a sign that something has returned, a tree
that has been set alight.

The empty place does not move, but because the others keep
going to stand somewhere else,
  The place disappears here and reappears there, as if it is moving.

The slightest thing I say becomes a net of desire
  To capture the fleeing empty place.

I could cry fire, wait to see which way they run,
  Then go in the opposite direction, a big fire behind me, my
shadow walking in front.

## In the Desert

I walk through the desert because I have to be somewhere.
   I saw mist when I woke up, mist in the desert—have you ever
seen anything like that?

If the Jews walk through the desert,
   Who will throw stones at them?

Someone walks through the desert,
   Crazy enough to think that if he can go back he will still be
able to go in a different direction.

The desert is narrow, there is hardly room to get past each other,
   For me and somebody else who can't get what he desires either.

## The Difference

The others hurried off in the middle of the night,
  But I left in the evening and walked into the desert far ahead of
them.

I didn't want to surrender that half day without getting something
in return.
  My lead only grew, after all I knew where they were going.

When I arrived at Mount Sinai, evening came, the shadows more
colorful than what cast them.
  At night I saw a fire high on the mountain, as if a man were
burning something.

The difference between what I saw and what I saw together with
someone I can discuss it with later,
  Or the difference between what I first saw alone and came back
to see together with someone else, which is greater?

## What's Your Name Again, the Only One Who Doesn't Have Any Plans for When Evening Comes?

You remember when you wanted to let me go on through the desert alone.

That was when I said I wouldn't let you go before you took back what you'd said.

Nobody can take back what he has said if nobody else is there with him.

That's what somebody close-by says, already dressed in his last clothes.

He can't stop listening to what he is saying, as if hearing himself when things could still have been different.

The best he can do is skip a few words and continue somewhere further along.

This is what Ghalib says about those who recite his poems,

In a way that has been chosen neither by Ghalib nor by those who recite them, but by those who recite the poems along with them.

You speak with someone else, you say that that is your name.

I ask if you would like something to eat because you might be one of those who does not give off any light to avoid disturbing the evening.

You sit down at the table, ask if anyone knows a poem, let everyone join in reciting the beginning, then say the end alone.

What I find more difficult is someone standing at the door and wanting to eat right away, as if he'll never get anything otherwise.

## Traveling to India

If someone lets me go in his place with his luggage, it is still his journey.
 Ghalib is too honest to take something from someone who is already halfway.

It surprised me the first time I heard it, but not later,
 Finding out that the world was round when I was traveling to India.

At night my ship didn't seem as small,
 In the middle of all that water, the sails filled with the wind to India.

I write this when I am so far away that the news I send back
 Will not arrive before everybody has forgotten who I am.

Ghalib, did you have to spend another day getting used
 To the idea that the stars you see at night might have disappeared long ago?

## A Joke of Ghalib's

Look, a circle on my skin where my heart is.
　　They say that I am like God because I can draw a perfect circle
by hand.

If the pen moves faster, I can make my hand heavier at the same
time.
　　My body no longer moves as fast as I would like it to when I
am imitating someone, that's why I need to become lighter.

When an angel moves, the surrounding air remains motionless.
　　The sound an angel makes is that of my pen on paper.

Can I still become someone who remains calm with what he has
so little of,
　　Who writes as if the ink is almost finished, some letters only
the imprint of the pen on the paper?

Ghalib, if you have given up all hope,
　　Why do you stand there waiting like a pauper in paper clothes?

## Arranging to Meet

If you would like to talk to me about the old days,
    We can meet at a café on the outskirts of town, even when it is
too cold, there are tables outside.

Don't worry, I won't make you wait.
    If you are already there you will see me coming in the distance,
the sky behind my head, we could have arranged to meet in an
empty bus shelter instead.

I would wait for you anywhere,
    As long as I can't see all of my supplies spread around me and
nothing being added.

We have not arranged to meet here at all,
    But I keep looking in all directions in case you come earlier
than expected.

I am startled to see how little you are asking,
    Yet sure you can't get it from me, there is nothing I can do
about that.

What we can arrange and what we cannot,
    Because if one of us doesn't stick to it, the other can't say
anything about it anyway.

Is this where God arranged to meet Moses? How should I know,
    Did one of them promise to bring something which they then
forgot and left behind here?

## A Joke of God's

I have to act like I am a friend from long ago, then they will let
me in right away,
    Just as I wouldn't want the first woman who had me counting
the hours until I could see her again left waiting at the door.

That's what I said to everyone who might try to stop you,
    And you don't have to bring anything for me, because what
could you give me when I already have everything?

If I die today they can burn my body or bury it,
    In the water, if it has been raining all day.

Do you really want me to tell you how I would like to be buried?
    What about lying on my back in a tub full of water?

Do you know how much I have written? Suitcases full!
    That's how I've worked out when I will die, by counting how
much I have written.

I make a small tear in the clothes I want to be buried in,
    And hope that when I die they will be the only clothes I have
left.

I walk cautiously where I think you have walked,
    Trying to see if your footsteps are visible in the grass, trying to
guess where you stood still.

I look for clothes you might have taken off one by one,
    As if walking to bed, the way I could have taught you, because
you said you wanted to learn from everyone.

Who else would I need new clothes for?

　　Not for the angel who half conceals himself in the grass when I approach.

I don't want to die far from here, where I will be buried as if I never had anything,

　　But if I can't count the hours until somebody comes, I would rather be taken to the door far from here.

This is one of God's jokes, something I can do in return:

　　When I die I will do it where nobody knows who I am, that will give God a solution for how poor I am.

Look what God has brought with him,

　　Like something an old dog has dragged in, does he think I will be grateful for that?

Ghalib doesn't get what he deserves, God said that long ago

　　It is good to remind you, Ghalib, that you once had a God.

Ghalib, there is so little to your poems that only you and God have the patience for them,

　　When you can sit together and talk about them, your whole life long.

## I Know Enough for a Novel

Something we can do when we have already done everything difficult,
    But I can do that now, saying something and hoping someone will contradict me?

We try to find a point from which something and something else seem to be the same for a moment,
    And then I say that I have forgotten where it was, weren't you going to mark the floor or one of the walls to show where it was?

It's easier if where I come from no longer exists.
    Others can walk around there and I know enough to keep them from constantly walking into walls.

Do I find it easier to breathe recalling what keeps increasing,
    Instead of longing to give away as quickly as possible what I still have left of what I had to give away?

You come to me and we read to each other: from a novel first, then history, then poems,
    Then a poem as a joke that doesn't make anyone proud.

I go to sit in the garden, you stay in the house.
    When you hear that I am finding it hard to breathe, you come out and take me by the hand, stroking my head with your other hand.

I would like to discuss this with someone who knows something about it,
    Like in the heavens, not where the dead are, but the empty sky.

If I don't know how to do something I would rather do it myself,
   Than have to listen to somebody else saying that what I am
asking is too difficult.

Can I watch how you do it once again?
   In exchange I will tell you that the shade of the one you long
for is still there, between the trees on the edge of the field.

## Smash Something on the Ground

When someone makes a small mistake,
    We immediately forget that he hasn't won, OK fine, we watch
him sitting there a little longer.

Sure, you can think you will win that easily,
    As if you are the only one who wants to win.

I have a few seconds to spare crossing the finishing line, enough to
raise my arms in the air.
    And what do I get for it, what did the one before me get?

Although it's a strange way to win if I have less afterwards than I
did before.
    You say, it's not a competition, it's your party.

A small mistake, like a small tear in my clothes,
    Which could rip further, in the clothes I keep wearing for days.

What happens every time I make a mistake?
    I say that this time I want to do as little wrong as possible, then
I will have to know a great deal.

# By the Door

Do you know who's standing at the door, one of the Jews who left Egypt in such a hurry.
   That's what happens if you want to do everything as fast as possible and you're not that fast.

I think of who I want to hear from, jump up and am glad no one can see me.
   I don't know how long you had been standing there when I looked back and saw you in the doorway.

You come to visit me and I open the door for you,
   Wearing the clothes of someone who opens and closes doors in your house.

Another trick: hiding between the door and the wall when the door opens inward.
   You come inside and can't find me.

A way of letting me in: you open the door and I walk in.
   Sit down on the floor somewhere, you don't need to say anything.

How do I know you are the best I ever had?
   Because I know you are coming closer while you are still far away, I can already go and sit by the door.

My workshop full of doors.
   I don't want to sell one because then it will end up somewhere where it's the only one.

I had just learned that the chance of something being somewhere does not depend on what I think.

Now I have to try to understand how changing my mind increases that chance.

## When I Hear Shouting I Can Shout Too

The dogs jump up and down and shout when someone walks
past, that's their job.
    They shout when they hear shouting, that's their job.

Shouting some more when the same person walks past again,
    Running after him if the gate is open, or is that how you lost
your last job?

A dog goes from garden to garden looking for work,
    But it can't say it's ever done it before.

Go ahead and shout, no one will hear you.
    Is that what you tell yourself?

This one is good at what it does,
    It only shouts once, that's all it has to do.

## Clothes

What I found out by washing and folding your clothes,
    They seem so small, though you're not much smaller than I am.

I turn clothes inside-out before washing them, who taught me
that?
    That's how you always take them off. If I find my clothes
inside-out I know you have been wearing them.

Do you see that nothing has happened, your clothes have been
ripped in half, that's all,
    But I'll drape them over you again, just stay still.

Come and get me, don't wait till tomorrow, I don't know what I
am doing here.
    Put your best clothes on so no one will stop you.

## Difficult, Possible

Today is a day to do exactly the same as the others, standing up and sitting down when they do.

It's alright if they see that I am copying them, they know I started later.

I don't need an explanation, but perhaps they can tell me where they are going afterwards.

Do I think a day will come, even if it is the day of judgment, when I will start something on time?

Today I heard good news, a day will come when no one needs to stay.

That will be my day forever, I'm curious who will be the last to tell me he is leaving.

We forgot to congratulate you, you received good news today.

You don't want to spread it round yourself, but it is possible to find out about it.

Walking through walls was difficult at first, but has become easier and easier.

Nobody believes it anyway, I am so bad at it they think the wall is not real.

The clothes I am wearing.

I couldn't look more like someone on a journey, but someone who will be back in a day, if he so chooses.

I try once again to do what others find easy, but for me it is difficult.

I am not pretending, it really is difficult, the first time I couldn't see how it was possible.

I can always think of plenty of reasons to leave me, I couldn't possibly get angry about it.

I have to get angry about it, but you don't do a better job of explaining why, that's advice not assistance.

I cried out for help, I smiled, I can't remember waving you goodbye.

Why I find it difficult to do something, because before doing something I want to have done it already just not for real.

But that is something that makes me feel colder, not warmer.

But that is something that makes it harder for me to breathe, not easier.

I come running and say: I can help make the day longer, that's not difficult at first, afterwards it's impossible.

Here the sun has disappeared, further along it's still there, run after me.

## Giving It Away

Maybe someone will buy it yet.
   If the offer for the whole package is ridiculously low, I can always give it away.

If someone only wants it if it's free and won't even come to pick it up, I can deliver it,
   Or wait here on the street,
         Keeping my eyes shut and hearing someone else's voice as I give it away to the person in front of me.

I've learned to sit on the street and sell
   What is now worthless to me because I have had bad news,
         Because you wanted to keep the good news for when I could be more generous.

If I see that someone wants something from me, I find it difficult not to hand it over.
   I act like it's not worth anything, as if that means that giving it away
         Has not weakened my position when I have to start negotiations.

I would gladly pay to make sure nobody can tell that, given the chance,
   I would like to receive news from so far away I could never go there.
         It's not like buying something, more like paying tax.

It's too late for me to learn to dance so well that they will shout good news at me.
   One day you will dance for me, not to show me what you have learned.

## Last Year there Were Three of Us

Alternate something with something else to be able to talk about two things at once.
　　Noticing afterwards that all it takes is the memory of one making you think of the other.

It is impossible to talk about something and nothing else.
　　The difficult thing is talking about one and the other at the same time and keeping it up.

If I find something difficult, I try to do something else at the same time.
　　I am doing so many things at once, I don't notice how slowly my hand is moving when I go to shake someone's hand.

I don't know if I am going to find something difficult until I have finished it.
　　I might have done something similar before, but I can't remember that step by step.

Last year there were three of us, now I am alone.
　　It has stopped raining, but if the wind comes by, drops fall from the trees.

Last year two others made my breakfast together.
　　In the morning one came down from the sky and the other climbed out of her hole in the ground.

In the evening, one there, the other over there, each in her place up in the sky,
　　Like two people who think of the same thing and say so out loud.

## How It Goes

I know how this goes, last time I didn't find a solution in time.
   But if I can try again I'll be more able to keep up with what's
happening—it helps to know a lot.

I will wait until I know so much I am able to decide, and if
something new emerges later,
   And I am no longer able to decide, someone else will have to
do it.

Longing for more than one person at once, so many I no longer
know who is who,
   And only dare call a name when they are all together.

I see one smiling, as if there are hundreds ready and waiting for
me to choose.
   What can I give forever to those I don't choose, they need to be
promised something too, don't they?

When I've counted them, how many fewer does it take to make
me change my mind?
   If one fewer, how many times?

I would like to see someone I longed for and never spoke to.
   There were times that was someone different every day.

If one of them was standing before me but didn't explain anything
to me, I wouldn't even remember having seen her before.
   If I only had two minutes left would you come and explain it
to me?

You don't know who I am anymore?
   I don't even remember if I ever promised anyone not to forget.

That's a joke, my longing for one and then the other, like so many times before,
   And falling asleep thinking of one on one side, up against me, and the other on the other, both still.

I still turn over a hundred times before falling asleep.
   What are they supposed to do, turn with me?

I no longer know how to move with others,
   Making what is too big smaller, making what is too small larger until we all move together.

If I were king I would have someone to make what I could long for.
   One day a year he would take my place, but I would not take his.

He begins or ends the day by choosing and if he prefers he can also delay choosing,
   What he has to choose between stays the same, what else can I offer him?

On the day of judgement God decides between the two of us,
   Which of us has to do what can still be done in what is left of that day.

Am I glad that today I can choose between this one and that one instead of just between yes and no?
   Ghalib, the more someone knows, the more explanations they need.

## A Storm

Starting the walls of the house deep in the ground,
  To raise them up high, so you can see the storm coming from
far away.

The money has run out, that's why construction has stopped, a
storm approaching over the water, that's why construction has
stopped,
  Ropes strung from the roof to the ground as if it were a tent.

A storm comes across the sea to the house on the coast that still
isn't finished,
  That does not yet have a roof or even all of the walls, maybe
there will be more left if the wind can blow through it.

The construction workers are standing in a café without chairs.
  Drink up, anything left will be wasted, or would I rather sit
down somewhere and wait for the neighbors to bring me
something to drink?

Is the oar on my shoulder for separating the heavy from the light?
  I stick the oar in the ground like a tree in the gentle breeze
blowing toward me over the water.

The light of the sun weakens as it descends, but just before it
sinks into the sea,
  Everything it falls on seems to be able to give back more than it
gets.

How many floors and a flat roof to sleep on when the night is
calm and the air inside the house is still hot.
  A storm in the garden, howling I run from tree to tree.

How many floors, ever higher,

 To see the mountains and the sea, more and more for the price of one, Ghalib, you are the specialist in the price of one.

## Ghalib and Muhammad

God asks two angels to make Adam from clay, the earth does not
want them to take it from her,
  The angels don't want to take anything she does not want to
give willingly, God asks the angel of death to make Adam.

The earth asks Muhammad if it's not too late for her to give what
she didn't want to give earlier,
  Because she can't bear having one dead person after the other
begin their unmoving wait inside of her.

An angel surrounded by clocks to tell him what time it is where I
am says,
  I can make you a proposition, like a salesman who is allowed to
sell as if he were the owner.

When he speaks I hear where he is from,
  Although he has practiced by keeping his words in his mouth
as long as he can in the dark.

There is someone who brings freedom when he comes,
  But he is no angel, and he doesn't know when he will be allowed
to come.

If someone can neither read nor write,
  He cannot come up with a poem as if it has been improved
from the beginning.

If you watch me while I am reading,
  I will not be able to improve your poem.

You tell me I have to read and don't give me anything to read, as if the first line is the last,

And I know how the last line must end, and recite it together with he who is reading it for the first time.

What it is like to be last is something only Muhammad knows.

Until I am last on the day I let everyone else go first.

# Free

Where has everyone gone, a minute ago there were thousands and
thousands of us.
    Have they all taken their share of what we have been given?

If so, how did they work out what my share was?
    Or is my share being free of an obligation?

I had forgotten how someone who was hiding could get free again,
    By running to where someone has his eyes closed before starting
to seek, or am I being too free?

I keep taking a step back, today or tomorrow I will arrive
somewhere I have never been before.
    Where I am now I don't even need the last thing I had, I can
keep it for later.

Is this all I can do? If you give me five minutes,
    Maybe I can learn something else as well.

Thinking about something as if it were five minutes ago,
    Or five minutes later, on its way to freedom.

I didn't even know how to get to the jail, I would never have found it
    If the prisoners hadn't gone out to stand near the entrance to
point out the last bit of the way.

They shout the whole day long, if it were quiet I could stay here,
    If I didn't make it more difficult by thinking about what I
could no longer do now I am not free.

# Here or There

I have to get undressed to show I had not planned what I wanted
to do in one world in the other,
    Sometimes I have to line up for days with all the others who
want to enter one or the other world,
        We move forward slowly, sometimes night falls and bright
lights turn on.

The ones who say who is allowed to continue and who is not are
children,
    They don't know what to watch out for,
        They make the one whose turn it is bend left, bend right,
stand on one leg.

Quickly I learn something new so I will be able to do more in
that other world than just the jobs nobody else wants,
    I will be able to walk around saying I can repair what is broken,
        Otherwise they would have to travel more than a day to
take it to someone who can repair it.

I know someone who loves it when you give him something to
repair,
    Without even having the tools others would demand before
starting,
        Maybe a short piece of string, is that any help?

Bring me to life, sit me down in a chair—I stand up and start
walking
        On the street someone shouts after me, gather up your
things, tie a string around them.

## Also Good

A barren plain full of monkeys, returned one after the other by their purchasers,
   Who wanted their money back first, then something else, and finally accepted just being allowed to leave the monkey behind.

There's the monkey I imitated when I wanted to look like a monkey, that one at the back, that was my monkey.
   It looks at me as if it still knows who I am and is wondering what I have done to it.

Give a monkey a suitcase, tell it it's going on a trip, watch what it packs,
   Inform it that it might not be coming back, watch how it behaves toward what it is not taking.

I know I just asked you for directions, and then walked off in that direction,
   And have now come back to ask directions somewhere else.

If I have found someone who can explain something to me,
   I ask him to explain something else as well, to see what is left of it.

Can he tell Ghalib, I will read it tomorrow,
   Because Ghalib sees so many things so clearly he will immediately think he can use it to understand something else.

**Hey, there's a difference between the chance afterwards and the chance beforehand. Oh, you mean you've done an experiment?**


If there were another world, I could do my experiments there.
    Not being able to think of a reason something would be there and not here is already enough.

In India there is a drunk man who never takes a step until he has forgotten where his previous step was going.
    How far does he get from where he started?

Unfair on whom? As soon as I am told there is something I can't do anything about,
    I want to know all about it.

If you need more time to say how to make something than to keep it,
    What do you know about it?

Ghalib wants to know things like that,
    Because he plays for money when he's in a hurry to pay off his debts.

## Words

I buy books I still want to read for when I am housebound.
　　When I was young I never managed to keep a book without reading it.

If you read a sentence and think it's the first time that word has been used like that,
　　Could you send me that sentence, or maybe the book it's in?

I try to guess which words will stick in your mind so that you still remember what they were referring to later.
　　I put them together to see what I can do with them.

I never buy just a single book, always boxes at once, preferably all the books someone has.
　　No, I am not a collector, I never have been, I just want a lot of something.

## And What We Do Then

I won't suddenly say afterwards that it was for real,
    As if the agreement was that I would only be paid if I did it
for real.

You could propose that what I say from then until then doesn't
count,
    Except when you say it does count and I agree to that.

I have discovered what I can work with,
    And I can also manage without, I discovered that immediately
afterwards, not bad!

What is it good for?
    One day someone will put a tax on it.

You have to find out for yourself what I should know
    To be able to say what you should do. I could tell you what I
would want to keep looking at for longer if I could see you.

Hey, I'm paying you two cents an hour,
    Reason enough for you to stop saying you're stupid and sad.

I change what I had promised to make every day.
    Every day someone could come to pick it up, I'll work it out then.

You know, that's something I am not very good at.
    This is not meant in my defense, but I have never met anyone
who was good at it.

## Pretty Boy

Being the pretty boy who fills your glass, is that my job?
   It's not an insult if you scream without looking at me that you
don't want to see the bottom of your glass.

If they hardly look at me when I enter a place where I have to be a
certain age,
   I can no longer say I am a boy.

It is easy to tell if I am saying something I don't believe.
   I touch my face with a finger, as if there's an opening there
somewhere.

A pretty boy watched you go past.
   You didn't even need to look round, someone told you about it
much later.

What it takes to make people look at a face,
   While it is changing its mind, with the light shining on it.

Sometimes this is enough, at other times much more is needed.
   That is still difficult to think about.

I don't think I was ever pretty enough to wait until morning,
   Next to where someone lay. I walked away before someone
came to see if he was still there.

You say that there were so many as pretty as me,
   On this morning that has already begun.

When Ghalib had the face of a man who, overflowing with love,
stopped for a moment
   Before walking on beyond the last houses,

He spent an afternoon thinking about whether he would do better to go and work in a factory in England.

Oh, Ghalib, you can look back over your shoulder so beautifully,
As if you want to ask something but don't, waiting for a moment before walking off.

## Abraham and the Two Angels

The sun high in the sky, God and two angels come to visit Abraham,
   Eating what he hurriedly prepares for them.

One of the two angels is Jesus, the other wants to be allowed to
walk through the streets of Jerusalem like Jesus.
   One of the two angels swaps places with Isaac, on top of the
mountain.

One of the two angels holds Jacob tight all night long, when it
doesn't count.
   When morning comes he walks away, Jacob sees that he can't
walk any faster.

## Which Mountain?

I have slept for a couple of hours in the middle of the day,
   And it is the one day on which it is possible that nothing
happened before this and nothing else will happen after it.

Just tell me which mountain it is, if it's the only mountain it will
not be difficult.
   High on the mountain, that's when it is difficult to be the only
one.

Does our agreement still hold? You were going to show me where
I had to go, where I can do what you are asking.
   I do what you say until someone else comes.

I sit at a table by the window and see a mountain, it must be that
one,
   And I try not to lose sight of it as I walk outside.

It is easy to see that it must be this one, it only has one tree.
Should I cut it down for firewood?
   But then there won't be any shade left in this high place.

## Abraham and Isaac

I have to choose, not choosing is also a choice.
   Or did I think someone else would come after who was willing
to take my place so I could go somewhere else?

When Isaac sets out with his father he is a child,
   And at the same time so old nobody would be surprised if he
didn't come back.

He has never gone anywhere alone. His father has promised to
teach him how,
   And how to negotiate when he doesn't have anything to offer.

Rain and lightning on a hot day, as an excuse in advance.
   Even on a hot day I like to wear something, old clothes full of
holes.

Ghalib, I think I now see how we can arrive at death,
   You and I, if we're early we can watch for a while.

# Abraham

Abraham apologizes, he has something else to say and knows that
he can't do it every day,
    And that it also counts if he doesn't say anything else after his
apologies.

If he would like to stay a night here, he can.
    That is the kind of offer Abraham can use to ask for something
else.

Abraham's part is that he always gets more of everything.
    He can also ask for it, but that is just a game.

Abraham's creditors can sell everything he owns,
    Then he can carry on as someone who is paid by his wife and
child, not for what he does, but by the day.

They can sell whatever he makes, even if he says it's not finished
yet.
    You would think it would get worse and worse, but it doesn't.

There will come a day when I will rent out the world, like
Abraham,
    An old man with a white cap on his head, two large circles
behind him on the wall.

This is Abraham who has walked down from high on the mountain,
    Because he is like an old man who thinks others are only
willing to listen to his apologies because he is a king.

## Leah Does With Her Tears What Rachel Does With Her Laughter

Purple and yellow flowers on the roadside,
    Beyond them high mountains,
        Is that all still Rachel?
    You mustn't see her naked,
        But you are allowed touch her, there's nothing wrong with
wanting to know what you're getting.

Marrying all of them,
    Like Jacob who worked
        For one daughter and got them all.
    He pretends it isn't so,
        But he can still tell
Rachel from Leah when they approach in silence.

# Joseph

Joseph is so beautiful he has to repeat his good advice three times
before anybody listens.
    He doesn't want to think any more about what else he could
have given good advice about.

If Pharaoh needs something, can he not take it from an earlier
Pharaoh,
    Who lies in the sun in the daytime and at night in a golden sea?

Joseph marries another of Pharaoh's daughters.
    Pharaoh says just because he has spoken to one of them he
doesn't need to immediately marry her.

Joseph sits at a table with the world's three best lovers.
    The waiter says he is serving wine to the world's four best lovers.

Joseph says the waiter can be as proud as he likes,
    But the others pay their women, his women don't even ask his
price.

If he talks to someone he doesn't need to go anywhere else.
    The waiter asks if that is so, how can a conversation with him
ever end.

A conversation ends when one of us remembers a poem by Ghalib
and recites it.
    Then even Joseph can stand up and walk away.

# Joseph

Half of all beauty goes to Joseph, the other half is shared over the rest of the world.

    This is my spring, nobody can tell me what my autumn is like when I make clothes of leaves.

Every shirt he wears takes on the smell of what cannot be bought back.

    His brothers all bought shoes with the money they got when they sold Joseph.

As beautiful as Joseph is,

    He is sold in haste, at a low price, over and over again.

How am I supposed to explain it to you if you can't remember something being too much to be yours?

    But instead of giving it away you wanted to earn something on it.

Joseph knows a lot about clothes, you can ask him if your clothes suit you.

    If you like, he will go to a store with you, to help you look for new clothes.

When Joseph takes off his shirt to give it to his brothers,

    The wind carries the smell to the old man in Canaan, as if the shirt is being laid over his face.

The smell from just one shirt makes it impossible for Jacob to breathe, and he wants to have them all.

    One is worth as much as all of them. How can I balance the books like that?

Would I like to have my clothes? Yes, I would like to have all of them.

What I look like naked, if I could choose something I would like to know in advance.

I am wearing my best clothes, but not for you. Nor for anyone else.

Do you remember, everyone walked away and the two of us were left behind?

## Joseph and Jesus

Joseph only says that he has dreamed something.
     Can't he think of a better dream than having the sun and the
moon and the stars gather round him?

If Joseph is asleep and two Jews come past, they will lift him up
and carry him into the desert.
     The next time they leave Egypt.

When I walk my feet make more noise, maybe I've put on weight.
     I can buy a new floor with money I earned and wanted to give
back, but they didn't want it anymore.

It is my own blood, if I don't want it to show anymore, I shouldn't
rub too hard.
     Otherwise I will make holes in my clothes or in the floor in
front of my feet.

Jesus weighs so much he almost sinks through the world with
every step.
     Joseph is so light people grab hold of his clothes when they
want to talk to him.

Jesus sells for a higher price than Joseph,
     But he is not more beautiful than Joseph, when Joseph was a
child he heard talk of that.

## Drinks All Round

Have you heard the latest news?
    The Egyptians have left Egypt to beat the Jews to it.

The reason he is alone?
    Because nobody wants to see him as he is, for fear they will not
be able to forget it.

I am no good for anything, but if it becomes clear that I am
staying with him,
    Others won't need to be afraid of being the last to leave.

As if yet again, something has ended differently from how
everyone thought I wanted it to,
    I enter and everyone is quiet.

Drinks all round, because I am leaving, is that not allowed anymore?
    Is it against the rules to all drink together when someone is
leaving, can they prohibit something like that?

There is no reason to leave,
    Except that I had heard that I was allowed to leave.

In a dream I am asked to give a speech—
    Fine, if I can leave immediately afterwards.

In the garden whose owner is absent, I can sit wherever I like.
    In the shade, although it is cloudy.

# Leaving Egypt

Magnificent uniforms, trumpets and drums,
    And what did we do with them, we sent them to war.

With an army like that we could have left Egypt,
    And a day later emerged on the other side of the desert, as if
thousands of idiots weren't getting in the way.

A general comes in; let him do what he suggests and soon you will
celebrate a great victory.
    If you keep waiting, I think it will not be possible later.

If you do it now, it will suddenly be as if everything you were
afraid of has fled before you,
    Clearing a path for you, you only need to follow along behind.

I have had what you have never had,
    And I know that I can never get it back, no matter how much I
want to, that makes it different.

This is your house, you will die somewhere here too,
    As someone says to Moses when night falls in the desert.

I wished I had something to offer you, like saying you can go back
to Egypt.
    Moses doesn't say that yet, but he practices it when he is alone.

If we stay close enough together,
    We can enter paradise like an army.

If we see someone, we will take him prisoner and demand a ransom.
   Enough to cover all of the ground we are standing on, as high as he can reach.

One of the Jews buries all his money before leaving Egypt,
   And every morning, as the others travel on, he buries everything he has apart from the clothes he is wearing.

I stay in Egypt, knowing that I will never again see those who leave tonight,
   But perhaps they can write me letters when they have found a place to stay the night?

## Nothing is Mine for Long

I lend money to others, and with them to yet others, it's not just passing it on.
 Too much always happens at once to be able to say where the profit is being made.

Have I forgotten how many decisions are mine when I am trying to be as free as possible?
 But I am free because I lend them to those who want to profit from them.

If somebody has stood before me to ask for money, I don't ask his shadow for interest,
 But for a share of the profits, never a share of the losses.

A monkey throwing darts at the stock market page in the newspaper will get rich faster than me.
 If the monkey makes a bad decision, it doesn't count its losses with the excuse that otherwise it won't learn anything from it.

Mirrors direct the light onto the paper on which the bookkeeper does his sums.
 If he makes a mistake, he pays a small fine.

I make a kite from paper and string and sell it to buy a parrot from the profits.
 The bookkeeper cannot explain how it works, not even with the parrot on his shoulder learning to do sums instead of talk.

I open a door when somebody wants to go from here to there and approaches quickly,
 And a door when somebody wants to go from there to here and approaches slowly.

In this way I enlarge the difference between here and there, that's profit, but not really,
    Because I have to add in how much it costs me to be able to say how fast somebody is approaching.

I don't forget what sometimes comes at me quickly and sometimes stays far away,
    But I do think that it might not be mine.

If I have to remember something to long for it, is it less
    Than not longing for what I remember, but counting the seconds until I can see it again?

## Making Money

I have never been able to make my money mowing lawns for longer than a day.

Though I have heard that you can make a lot of money off it, like you can delivering newspapers.

I would be afraid that later I would make as much in a day as I would have made then in a year.

If I don't tell anyone what I can be congratulated on today, how can anyone guess it?

I would do better to put it in the paper and take it round door to door myself,

Because the paperboys have made so much money they no longer want to get up early in the morning.

Have I stopped saying morning in the morning? If I don't even want to do that, I shouldn't show myself.

I shouldn't say it's to make money, I don't see any hats to throw money into.

For years I made my money searching for birds I hadn't read about,

Taking them with me when I sailed home.

In the middle of the ocean the captain comes to tell me the ship is on fire.

I am only allowed to take as much as I can hold in my hands.

I can make something ten times as big, like the biggest ship ever built.

Nothing can stay the same but only get bigger, and it will be easy to see if a mistake has been made somewhere.

From the lifeboat I see one of the birds drowning.
    I lift it up out of the water,  am I supposed to throw it back?

There is no better way of looking at what is high above the world
for just a little while,
    Than lying on my back in a small boat in the middle of the
ocean.

If you no longer want to see me, am I allowed to find it terrible if
it also costs me money?
    When I walk through a desert I always keep my pockets full of
money,
        In case I encounter someone who wants to borrow it
from me.

To pay one, I borrow from the other, and one day I ask myself
why they can't do that themselves,
    Taking ever greater amounts from one to the other and back
again,
        More and more, because of interest and penalties, there's
money to be made there.

Ghalib dies and hasn't paid his debts,
    Unless you take advising his creditors to keep him alive into
account.

## Later You Can Say You Shook His Hand

If I think that I am the first to know that summer or evening is
coming,
    What can I think of to sell?

But if the price has gone down and I think it will go down further,
    I don't want to sell everything.

I wanted to sell what I didn't have,
    Because I thought the price would go down.

If I have borrowed more than I can ever pay back,
    A day will come when they will make me a proposal.

Ghalib has lost more than anyone.
    If I saw a child standing in the corner of the same room I
would take it by the hand to lead it over to shake his hand.

## In the Distance

When I know enough I can get by without music in the distance.
    I would believe it if I couldn't hear music in the distance,
what's more I know the music.

The one who has stayed with me for a long time
    Now leaves me alone—I don't hear it, but others can tell from
the music in the distance.

Because I remember what it was like, I know a way to make you
stay.
    Tell me you would like something, then I will have to give it to
you.

Who should be thankful to whom that who keeps revolving
around whom?
    As if I don't know that everything revolves around everything,
further and further away.

Regarding Ghalib, I know that he has written a magnificent poem,
    I would like to see what else he has written a few years later.

## Ghalib at Work

Stop boasting, you don't have that much work at all, it's evening
and you haven't turned any lights on.
　　If that's your work, how bad at it can you be?

If I've finished my work, I am given more work.
　　That's why I work as slowly as possible, but they push me
forward and say, do your work.

You see me doing it and explain how I can do it better.
　　Maybe I wanted to do it without having to do it well.

I don't mind having instructions I can't follow shouted at me the
whole time,
　　Because I am not fast enough and having a better understanding
of what I need to do only makes me go slower.

If I remember more than I have ever done, I am allowed to go and
stand where it is too narrow for others to get past me,
　　Or in the middle of a plain, they walk past me left and right,
that's how slow I can be.

Ghalib, who was your teacher? You give a name nobody knows.
　　Later you admit you made it up when you didn't dare tell them
how you learned to write.

The most ridiculous thing that has ever happened.
　　They ask Ghalib if he also made up who taught him desire.

I have already had so many instructions and I think I will not be getting any more.

Ghalib looks like he is being given an instruction like the ones he used to be given, in the middle of a long series of instructions that led him to his work.

## Ghalib and His Career

Ghalib decides to pursue a career in the service of the British queen.

Not in her army, though his grandfather once silenced a line of soldiers by riding toward them on his horse.

Perhaps as an official who rides through his province with two tents.

When he sits down in front of the first tent early in the morning, the second is already on its way to where he will be that evening.

If there is at least one great poet who has written in English, Ghalib can learn that language easily.

Send him a book of his poems, translated into Persian, so he can improve the translations.

The queen needn't worry, he has thought about how to make sure he has a long career.

Ghalib wants to find out who is the best living English poet and who is the second-best.

The second-best English poet leaves his house after dark and keeps walking.

When morning comes he says where he lives and asks which direction it is.

The best English poet receives dozens of letters every day from rose growers.

He has asked them to let him know if they see something they have never seen before.

Ghalib wants to write to him as well to answer his questions.

But what about? Would he like to know what the flowers looked like in paradise?

He becomes a gardener who wants to tend the roses until they turn red.

When it gets cold at night he brings the flowers in.

The other officials complain if they have to write a report at the end of the year,

But Ghalib writes letters to his queen all day long because he wants to tell her every one of his decisions.

## Practicing

How do I get from here to where I have to wait before continuing?
    Practice hard!

You know, I could take a sentence from the end of a begging letter
I wrote
    And use it in the middle of a poem.

Could you give me something,
    But not something you were going to give me anyway, only later.

If you can give me a comparison like the ones that only Ghalib
can make,
    As practice for something else, I would sit down on the street
and practice.

## Another Angel That Works Every Day

Before someone is born, an angel comes and brings him to life.
    If the angel fails again, he leans the dead body against one of
the walls between which he does his work.

The way I faint in a dream, with my head against a wall,
    Remaining on my feet, but with my knees bent as if about to
kneel.

When he was starting and heard that he would never get a day off,
    God asked him how far away he wanted the walls.

Fortunately he said he wanted them further away than the stars.
    Just say when, otherwise I won't know what you mean.

## Do You Want To Hear This?

You ask me for money and when I've given it to you and walked on, you run after me to tell me your name.
   If something proves difficult one day, I can ask for your help.

I try to guess how much I can ask for.
   I have learned that it's better to make a proposal.

Spinning round and swinging my arms as if learning to dance.
   If I also think about how I'm going to say something while dancing, I have to laugh.

I keep my eyes shut while turning slowly on the spot. In a minute I'll guess which way I'm facing.
   If the auctioneer takes it as a bid, it cannot possibly be a high bid.

I have heard that everything being sold today
   Has been taken from those who couldn't pay their debts.

Ghalib always wants to hear about new ways of selling something at auction,
   Like when the second-highest bidder has to pay something to the highest bidder.

## Water

There is enough water near my house
    To spend every day sitting somewhere I haven't been for a long
time.

A procession passes on the river, ship after ship, almost entirely
above water.
    I would like to be taken somewhere like that.

You have made a profession of crying because someone has died
without leaving you anything.
    At least there is no doubt about what you are selling.

When I am being taken away over the dark water,
    You will be standing on the bank, quiet as I pass.

## And what are we going to do then? Can I write that on the wall?

I learn to write by tracing letters with my finger.
　　I already know the letters, but want to learn to write them
again this way too.

I stand on a bed and write on the wall,
　　Jumping up and down on the bed to get the first words as far
up the wall as possible.

The moon in the sky like a letter from a box of letters,
　　If I might not have any time left to learn to write.

When it's too dark to see the paper and I don't want to turn on a
light,
　　I write in ever bigger letters, spaced far apart.

## How Someone Is Made Whole Again

I change into an animal that will be slaughtered
   By the one whose other hand will be held by the one who
could not yet come that day.

If nobody eats meat anymore it won't stop it.
   Those who are allowed to slaughter animals will take one into
their home to slaughter if they can.

The animals are standing in kitchens, close to the smell of food,
   Or leaning against walls that are white, gray in the shade.

If someone is too slow he finds himself in an empty house,
   Writing on a wall and erasing it again with the sleeve of his
shirt.

## Standing Just in Front of a Wall to Ask Questions

I wanted every question I was asked to consist of different parts,
    Not like a wall made of the same bricks laid on top of each
other.

Because I wasn't asked any other questions today,
    Or no questions in parts, which could be split up further,
something I was allowed to do myself.

The Earth is close and from heaven they can see when it is night
there.
    In heaven Moses sleeps every night in a different house without
walls.

I can't say how far away this or that is.
    I wanted to have a wall that looked like that, because it helps to
see something else the same way.

I am slowly getting better at remembering what the sky above
looks like
    Each time I become more free because something is possible.

## Investigated and Confirmed

Perhaps I would do better to grow a beard like an Assyrian king's,
    A wide beard, trembling brows, lashes, lips.

A woman with a newborn babe can walk from one end of the
kingdom to the other,
    That's how powerful the king is.

The king of Assyria hunts lions that have been brought to the
field in a cage.
    I hold up what I want to show them, my head by the hair, it's
well worth it!

Riddled with arrows, the lions lie on the ground,
    On their backs or their sides, holding themselves tight by
wrapping their front legs around their bodies.

I once read somewhere that men without beards are stupid, that's
why I stuck a false beard on my face,
    So long it stopped me from falling asleep in bed, that's why I
burned off half of it.

# Enough

I have seen no more of the one who said that if he had a second life it would be mine.

    I wished I had seen more of the one who made morning for himself, who said my morning.

He can build his own house, he doesn't make day or night until the house is ready.

    His legs spread, a hand on each knee, that's how he sits on a chair in the doorway. There is no door, he doesn't know how to make one.

Something that might just as well not be mine, would anyone else want it?

    The day's last sunlight is enough for me, profit and loss are enough for me.

I take off my shirt in the shade of a tall tree, yet the sun doesn't shine here often.

    Seeing a large ship and an even larger ship just behind it: if that is a ship, what is *that*?

It is evening, so I think of the evening I have already made. May I leave now, I don't need to be here yet?

    It is a rare thing, happiness without pain, just being there is enough for me.

## Mirrors

A shadow over a shadow like a hand on a hand in the shade of a
tree,
　　Like a face on a face in a mirror.

Covering everything with mirrors,
　　So you can no longer lose anything, if you look quickly you
can see yourself somewhere no matter where you are standing.

Stars and clouds in a mirror.
　　Let's throw away another thousand years like that.

I saw that one coming for so long I hoped it would just keep
going,
　　But it stayed here quietly for a while with me.

# Ghalib and Jesus

If they noticed that another man had taken his place, they would go in search of Jesus,
   Releasing the other man, but they crucify him first.

Jesus travels through Persia to India, stopping in a village by the sea.
   They don't beat him, but he is hungry and when he walks by the sea he is cold.

It is not easy to make you beautiful, you are so small and slight.
   I want to take you to the seaside for a second and last visit, to look out at the low waves.

Small children who are already too fat to stand up unaided,
   But promise them something they really want and they will run along the beach.

In a dream I hear a voice telling me that I will soon be going back, the ship is ready.
   I must walk naked until I reach the sea.

Maybe there's a piece of wood on the beach I can sit on, paddling with my hands,
   Moving slowly through still water, no waves except the ones I am making.

I am working on an apology for more than one wrong decision at a time, like Jesus.
   I am sorry that I drank your glass half empty and then the other half too.

As if I thought of something yesterday and lost the piece of paper I wrote it down on.

The animal the butcher passed over ate the animal that had eaten the piece of paper.

Jesus's lips move, but without a sound, breathing for someone else, that was Jesus's trick.

Ghalib can do that too, that's why they call out for him so often.

# Excuse

When you suddenly want to even up, between you and me, but
what's five cents between you and me?
    When it comes to money I always get scared, is that my excuse?

I thought you were not that poor, but now I see
    That you really are poor, I apologize.

Today I will make the words as calm as possible,
    Then there won't be any excuse if they make people cry, they
would be rich if they could sell what they have been given.

There already being a world, is that my excuse for not making
one?
    And notice that I do not say: allowed to long for—that's not
something one can allow or disallow.

I know the excuse for doing this and don't need it.
    Today I can do this because there is nothing else I long for.

I walked in the wrong direction again,
    And again I arrived a day early, what's my excuse?

We had suggested so many different days to each other,
    Although I admit that I am the one who forgot what we finally
agreed on.

## The Old Man with a Dog

The old man with a dog says, I have a question for you,
    Can you tell me what kind of dog this is?

We're standing on the street, it's cold and the sun is shining. The
man says he wants to go back home.
    He says he would never let someone like the one he once saw
walking by my side leave him.

Where am I now: at feeling cold because I am shivering,
    Or at the place where one and the other are not yet fully
arrived but still seeking each other?

Did I see someone walk past? With a hat on his head?
    An old man? No, I haven't seen anyone like that walk past.

Every day an old man walks past the place where the one who
stayed with him for a long time said yes to him,
    To breathe in some of the air,
        I am that easy.

## Something Else

When I was a child I could have pretended I was sleeping next to someone I loved.

Perhaps later I would have needed less nights to learn how.

All the things I shouldn't have done when I was a child, didn't I have anything else to do then?

Every night I tried to imagine what it would be like if I loved someone, isn't that enough?

If I can say that I am so slow I always arrive late, then I have something.

If I can say that there are more examples than necessary, I can take one back.

My father said it helped to think of something I can look at for a long time,

A sailing ship on the water for instance, or whatever I can look at for a long time.

Poetry is the creation of meaning, nothing else.

Each time Ghalib thinks up a new meaning, God wants him to exchange it for something else.

A poem brings the day of deciding closer, a dream about a poem gives a day's respite.

Where words mean something, Ghalib's are law.

## Any News?

I had wanted to bring along someone who gets further than me.
Not every time he wants to, but often enough that he can remember the last time as if it just finished.

I had wanted to bring him with me to your place, so he could see that there is also something I won't give up readily.
Or so you would see it, I'm not afraid of showing how little I have left.

I want to introduce you to someone.
He can give up in a way I can't, as if the one who wanted what I asked for was someone else.

You talk to me as if I am no stranger,
And the following night you comment with surprise at my being there again, where have I been all this time, you thought I didn't want to come anymore.

It's almost morning, does anyone want to buy a newspaper for you?
The boy who delivers newspapers on his bike will surely sell one if he gets enough in return.

If you ask for something small I am allowed to do it, but if it's important I am only told later,
Because I still get frightened when something is beginning.

## In Paradise

There are so many kinds of fruit in paradise and flowers that
don't all bloom at once,
    But I have seen the faces of the dead,
        And seen that they are as they are alone, but with less to
decide about, not more.

For instance two of the dead decide if they want to stay together.
    They go to an airport and drink something in one of the bars
in the departure hall.
        Nobody pays any attention to them there and it is well lit.

If I can remember that I worked for an angel for a day,
    I can enter paradise while I am still alive,
        And early in the morning walk the street where angels live.

Angels get frightened when they see a horse that only starts
running when the race is almost over,
    Because they think it is two men in a costume,
        But, you know, it's like the other horses are waiting for it,
as if they don't want it to be over yet.

A horse balks at something that frightens it.
    I mustn't start shouting, because then it will remember the
shouting every time it sees it again.
        I would do better to dismount, guess what has frightened
the horse and carefully touch it.

I know, for you, it's an important decision. Can I offer you
something to drink?
    Say what you would like, we have almost everything.
        You can't feel anything here unless you learned it long ago.

If you make the wrong decision you still won't be doing worse
than me, ready in my best clothes for I don't know what,
    If I can't choose one of two, but one of I don't know how many,
        I've already written down my decisions, I'm just waiting
for the one I can make those decisions about.

## You Know

The night is almost over when I go to bed.
   You would make me happy if you came to me while I kept my
eyes shut.

You know, I still have everything I had, when I came to deliver it
you were nowhere to be found.
   What an exaggerated way of confusing me, someone who even
gets lost in the dark.

If I come to you, go away from you, evening and morning, quieter
in the morning,
   The best comes at the end, we have both always done well from
it.

Going to bed I put on half of my clothes on top of each other.
   Maybe you can help me to take them off and put on the other
clothes.

I don't know a lot about going somewhere, but buy clothes I will
never wear.
   I don't know a lot about you, but you tell me you will tell me
more.

# Welcome

At night the bird dealer puts the cages in a garden.

That's what he says, but he puts the cages on the street or in a corner of a vacant lot.

The birds in the cages welcome other birds to the garden.

Not wanting to deprive the birds in the cages of anything, they don't contradict them and spend the rest of the night with them.

Going to sleep at the end of a hot day in a garden or a park,

I promise that next morning it will look as if nobody has ever slept in it.

I wake up on a park bench around noon—the sun has disappeared and the sky is gray.

If something happens and I need more time, who will give it to me?

I fall asleep in the afternoon at a table by the open window, my head on my arms.

I wake up surrounded by petals that have blown in.

How am I to explain this to the bird that comes to the garden when it gets dark?

The new arrangement was that it wouldn't stay the night, but only come if it were filled with desire.

## Flowers

I am free to leave whenever I like, I don't need to take anything
with me,
    Not even what I have been given.
        If I have been given flowers I am free to say, keep them
yourself, you are better at that than I am.

I get a bunch of flowers and forget to put them in water,
    Carry them to a corner of the garden to lay them down there,
        Petals everywhere, as if I'm scattering them for someone
who is following me.

A bird thinks that a rose is a bird
    That is not real because a real bird is never that beautiful,
        Put there so it will sit down next to it.

The only thing the bird can do is make the flower laugh,
    Like the smallest boy at dancing lessons,
        His face next to the breasts of whichever girl he is dancing
with.

I don't get flowers when I leave,
    I get them when I arrive and hold on to them,
        A bunch of flowers when I am standing at a door and
everyone knows I know nothing about flowers.

We are still where we are,
    Writing poems is still the same,
        What shall we agree, to always dress according to the
latest fashion?

I don't know anything deeper than that,
  Otherwise I might just as well talk about flowers or something
else I know nothing about.

Birds fly figures of eight in the sky, always higher or lower or at
more of an angle,
  As if a dancing teacher is saying, use the floor!

I travel far away to say this, I always have to take the longest route
back,
  The only thing that doesn't change is how to write poems,
    I dreamed I heard this, I would have had to be deaf not
to hear it.

## On This Day a Year from Now

On this day a year from now, I won't need to pretend
    I am giving myself what I want to receive, as if I need to act it
out.

Nobody asks me for something, as if they guess I will want too
much in return.
    I could also spend half a day going far away and half a day
coming back.

I pay half and you pay half, or you pay for this and I pay for
something else.
    Or I pay everything if you don't have anything left, but I would
rather you didn't say that.

I got half yesterday, I'll get the other half today.
    Or did I not realize yesterday that it was only half?

If I am asked to do something I'm not good at,
    I can ask if I can work half time, just getting by on half pay.

If I am still alive on this day next year,
    Will I hope I can stand still there, exactly where something ends?

Walking back and forth, saying the things I have heard out loud.
    How else can I cope with longing for how I was?

When I was allowed back because it was stormy, who could I thank?
    I didn't need to pay for anything while waiting until I was
allowed to go back.

## What Kind of Day

What kind of day, what kind of evening is it?
  It stays light so long I no longer know whether it's day or evening.

When I go to visit I stand still on the street and wait
  Until someone comes out to ask if I would like to come in.

After all, I am the one who conquered Persia,
  And thought in India that he had come to the end of the world.

Ghalib gets the newspaper from Persia.
  He doesn't need to run out onto the street if there is unexpected
news.

## Because Ghalib is What?

Because you are the king of Persia,
    You are standing in a walled garden in which all of the world's
flowers grow.

If you notice that a flower is missing,
    You have to go and conquer the country where that flower
grows, yet another victory.

Because you are the king of all India you are allowed to wait in
the shade of the wall of a house,
    When the sun is so high there is almost no shade left.

How you conquered India? You pretended to attack and then you
pretended to retreat,
    And then you gave a sign to your reserves in hiding.

You are thinking of joining the British army.
    There is no other army nearby, you can learn how they do it
and later start for yourself.

Ghalib, aren't you scared that they will make you a general right
away?
    Then you will have to stay for at least a couple of days.

## Ghalib, would you like to know how India is governed?

A man who is almost naked walks to and fro in his office.
  He sits down when he is able to write down another decision.

By early afternoon he is finished for the day and can go do
something else.
  When he was a child he already knew everything he needed to
know to govern India.

It frightens him to think that he would not feel any better
  If everything he could propose had already been done, would
you like to know how he dies?

Maybe you would like to know how he loves first?
  He thinks that if there had been more like her, the earth would
have become like heaven long ago.

The birds in his garden follow the doctor who told him he was
dying,
  From tree to tree as he walks to and fro in the garden.

## The King When It Is AlreadyDark

Give me something that cannot stop at any moment.
   Music that doesn't make me want to go back.

When I heard music for the first time, I thought one piece of
music would be enough.
   Now I put off listening to music until it can be different from
how I remember it.

You ask me to play some music for you.
   I ask if I am allowed to wait on the palace roof until evening.

The palace roof is higher than all the other roofs.
   If I pace to and fro there, nobody can see how long everything
I do takes me.

This is an evening I was given as a gift.
   I don't need to do anything except what I can do alone.

When I was king I thought it was just for a day,
   That it would stop before it began to grow dark, it was already
clear that it would soon be evening.

In my mind I hear what I wanted to listen to,
   I thought it had already started but it is still quiet.

It frightens me how fast I forget who is with me.
   You are quiet and when you start to talk I think you have been
talking the whole time.

I stand at your door when it is already dark.
   Tomorrow I will no longer be king, do I want you to quickly
do something for me?

I sit on your bed, the only thing in your house that is higher than the floor.

  I ask you for what I myself have said I no longer want, you calling someone back to speak with them.

A youth arrives who is as beautiful as Joseph when he dreams out loud.

  And I say, No, not him, the old man who said I am the king.

## Waiting

When the wine sellers see me they fill a glass with what they have been keeping
    For the day they stop waiting for what they most desire and I don't ask if they can lower the price.

We agree to invite each other to drink something together when one of us is no longer with us.
    A little later you are already no longer with us, I invite you and you come as agreed.

Suddenly I *am* able to be a good host, drinking together with you without hurrying.
    If there are two ways of waiting, can I give an example of each?

I can go to a store in the middle of the day and wait my turn,
    Or I can go early in the morning and wait on the street until the storekeeper arrives to open the store.

I don't know much about wine, that's why I ask for as much as possible.
    After all, someone who knows a lot about something only needs a little.

If I didn't drink so much, you would think I was someone who didn't need anything,
    Except an empty spot in front of my feet as long as I am walking.

What frightens you, Ghalib, when you do what you see others doing,
    It doesn't take long before you start waiting until you can stop again.

# Night

I thought it would be busy, but only a few people have come:
    Abraham and Moses, Jesus and Joseph, me when I was a child,

And it is already late at night, I don't think anyone else is coming.
    Shall we all say goodbye together or one by one, and whose
turn is it to go last?

Night also means leaving on a journey when the night is almost
over.
    No longer thinking about how I can be a guest but about how
to welcome a guest,

Who walks in the street as long as it is night, calm and as if
drunk.
    If anybody sees her, point her in the direction of Ghalib's house.

## Work for Me

I wanted desire to fill me in the same way,
    As if I had a job, a real one, for which I was paid every day, and
which I had just lost.

If I drop something and it breaks, it is not enough for me to pay
the price.
    I have to buy it again myself, but maybe you can't get it anywhere
anymore.

If I don't know who to ask for help I make mistake after mistake,
    Like when I broke into a palace and only took things nobody
wanted to buy from me.

The day the poor start to help each other instead of fighting over
every little thing that falls among them,
    Will be the day I have fallen among them as if from on high.

The sun shone all night when I went out to sell lamps, I knew in
advance that it would do that.
    That's why I said a night would come when I would have no
lamps left to sell.

Because the year is almost over, I receive a gift, everyone who did
the same work as I did receives the same thing:
    Permission to light fireworks before it gets dark.

## The Last Day

The night before the last day he held the hand
   Of the only other person left.

He can't say something like that as an excuse
   If he wasn't where he was expected to be one evening.

On the last day the same angel comes to kill him and raise him up
again.
   He has to bury him too, who else is going to do it?

He is waiting in a cemetery to make sure everything goes as fast as
possible.
   That's not necessary, says the angel, there are open graves
everywhere.

He doesn't have to worry about being late,
   Jesus will only come after he has had his turn, and then it will
get dark.

When evening comes, Jesus is standing before God.
   The angel that found him where he was lying says that once he
was back on his feet he wanted to cut down the first tree he saw.

When it has grown dark, Muhammad arrives, he is always last,
   Unless Ghalib has found an excuse to make them wait even
longer.

## Another Way

Once I have become rich, it will not be difficult to become poor again.
   If the price of something rises, I will buy more of it.

Because they are unable to say no to you, they sell everything when they hear you are coming,
   But I am not worried, the way prices are falling, I will soon be able to buy everything you could ask for.

I want to go to your house and pick out something that reminds me of you,
   The others who long for you could offer me that.

I will skip the things they have left notes on saying they would like to have them themselves,
   And also anything that could make someone who sells it later rich.

I know another way to earn money quickly,
   Making a bet about whether that man would pay his debts if I walked up to him and told him tomorrow is the last day.

I give him the chance to be like someone talking to someone else on a ship that is disappearing under water by saying,
   Here, this is what I owe you, now we are even.

Providing a feast for beggars who never ask for anything.
   They wash in the river and are given new clothes and plates of food.

They want their old clothes back, but they are not allowed to go and get them.

In the distance they see their clothes being burned.

In the burnt remnants there is enough money to pay for the feast three times over.

A proud man, whoever thought of this.

How I imagine another world when I consider how many of them there are.

Evening comes, the sidewalk is full of people, those walking in the same direction as me are going much faster or slower than I am.

It keeps getting darker, I can hand over what I have with me, it is all I have,

Or accept what I am given by those who stop in front of me, preventing me from going further.

If God can make more than one world, there must be someone in each world who is last.

You can get rich if you can say what to do on the last day.

That is something I've never done: walking past something that isn't for sale

And asking if it's for sale, as if I am ten times as rich.

If I am the last one who has become poor, they ask me

What it is like to still be able to get richer because everyone wants to do what I ask for almost nothing.

A rich child walks through a poor village as it grows dark,

Shouldn't he have been put to bed long ago?

There is the child who is told that he never says anything without a reason,

He has walked through a desert and crossed a sea in a small boat.

## Come and See

A cold night and a storm, I don't need to be naked, I can also get dressed.
   I still know a lot, but what would I like to be the last thing I forget?

I am squatting on a windowsill,
   As if I learned as a child to move in that direction when I heard something that frightened me.

It is almost finished, yesterday I left it lying there like that on purpose.
   I still hadn't worked out how to do the last bit, but thought that I would only need to look at it once to see how.

Being allowed to look because it is the last time.
   Led here by the arm so I could keep my eyes closed until then.

You are right, I am not speaking to you like a friend.
   If I ask for something it is always the last of what is left.

They came to watch because the last thing that could happen to him was going to happen to Ghalib,
   But there was nothing to see and nobody came to tell them it had been canceled.

# Ghalib and God

God is ahead in the competition between God and me,
    But he also started before I even existed, that's the kind of
player he is.

I'm not even talking about the competition who can stay together
the longest,
    And the only competitions I take seriously are the ones I'm
prepared to lose to you.

God only says that it took him days to make the world,
    But it was only the amount of time he needed to forget someone.

Take a good look at these clothes, feel how soft the material feels,
    And then look at the stars, but because they were made by God,
nobody dares to say anything.

I see someone burning his own clothes.
    He can't be doing it to stay warm, what does it smell of?

Ghalib, you talk about the competition we have with God,
    He has left an opening in his defense, that way he knows
exactly where we will appear.

How bravely we walk forward, each of us deserves a medal,
    And God is going to pin them on our chests.

Ghalib can't get to the end of the day without feeling warm and
cold at once,
    Then he can't go any further and stays lying there where nobody
can come and help him.

## Night and Morning

Answering questions as well as possible.
   That's being honest, isn't it, at least with the last question of
the night?

Did I think a day would come when I would only be honest?
   When I could not go away again? I thought there would be
another question.

Above me hangs a lamp,
   As if I will answer all their questions if they keep me awake
long enough.

Shall I sell clothes to the dead, going from door to door,
   Or sell lamps where it is dark?

You live there? One of those lit windows in the dark?
   How can the light be on, you are right here?

How am I supposed to know you leave the light on when you go
out?
   I admit, if there were a burglar in your house he would not
turn on the light.

The lamp that shines all night becomes invisible when morning
comes,
   Because it gives exactly the same light as morning.

# In the Dark

I dance like a bear in a long coat with pockets: one for letters I
still have to answer,
   One for coins—that makes me a bear that jingles.

On the night of my wedding they take me to a dark room.
   My bride is already there. They push me in and close the door
behind me.

We grope along the walls in search of a door and go outside
where it is dark.
   From that day on, I only visit you at night, as if nobody's
allowed to know.

One day we will say if we want to be together in the daytime,
   And if we want to be quiet in the dark.

What are you doing, Ghalib, besides saying what it is like here
once again?
   As if someone in the dark wants to hear that.

## End of the Night

I have never been where the sun is like a lamp behind a sheet of
thin fabric,
    But I know the color of the fabric and I know the valuables,
wrapped in the fabric.

The arrows, wrapped one after the other in velvet, in the velvet-lined
sheath,
    The bow, unstrung, wrapped in velvet, the oiled string in a
linen cloth, the archer asleep, naked.

I have to knock on all the doors early in the morning,
    But they know I am no longer able to do it, that's why they
brought me all their doors last night.

Waking up early while the night is still in a hurry to tidy up, I
don't often dream of home anymore.
    The sun appears, and others who must have been awake for a
long time too are out walking, they can't have come out of thin air.

What I say about myself remains true even if I leave today and
never come back,
    I am like that, what would you like me to say something about?

Standing in my room, I want to lie down and there is no bed.
    I could yell, frightening anyone who knew I didn't have a bed.

I write down once again how I want what is mine to be shared out.
    After all, that is the beginning of writing and the reason I
learned to write.

Someone who sees what I have written thinks I haven't slept.

The door is not shut, the door has gone outside, my bed went outside days ago.

Then I will cope with only having half.

If I were to get the other half now, too, it would be like losing something I had never had.

I have enough water to drink and to fill a bath for the birds.

The night is almost over when the birds fly off without having been anything other than still with longing the whole time.

Do I collect days or nights? That is the question Ghalib asks.

Every time someone hasn't waited for me it becomes night, when I sweep the nights together it is morning.

## A Joke of Ghalib's

What is it when something seems to stop and turn back but
actually continues on?
    I recognize it happening, but I don't know what it is,
        Although I think it's something you learn in the first lesson,
and if it's too difficult for you, you're better off doing something
else.

When I don't have anything to do one afternoon, I climb a
mountain that's too difficult for me.
    I don't want to shout for help, so I shout something else,
        Because I can't continue up or go back down.

I always say yes if you ask me to walk ahead to the other side of
the garden.
    If it serves a purpose, you follow me.
        One of us has to reach the other side, even if the sun is in
our eyes.

I wanted more to be easy because I had already started doing it
before stopping with something else.
    It's still difficult, but if it was up to me,
        It would be like a child who doesn't yet know how to tell
a joke or at least this joke.

Do I need to explain what a street is?
    You're standing somewhere and there are rows of houses left
and right as far as the eye can see,
        And the setting sun lights the top floors of the houses on
one side.

Teaching a bird to dance with a mirror,
  By feeding it the mirror bit by bit like sugar,
    And when it looks in the mirror, it can see you moving.

## Ghalib Knows So Much

The drunk dancing girl spins around, catching snowflakes—I'm working too, she shouts.
If you ask now, I will come to you. If you don't ask me to stay, I will leave again.

I walk across in front of you while covering your eyes with my hand.
Once I am past and my hand has slid off your face, you are allowed to look.

If you come with me, you don't have to go with anyone else,
As everything I can possibly know is already someone else's memory.

I didn't know I could talk like that, with big leaps to what I want to discuss,
Crossing a dark field surrounded by frozen ditches.

This is no dance competition, facing the same way while we leap and turn,
Our shoes landing on the dark earth, the thin layer of ice on top and the dark earth beneath it.

What kind of shoes would you buy if you had my feet?
I can do anything you can do, I follow your every movement, in the air, otherwise there wouldn't be room for both of us.

I am with you, but I leave you alone for the last bit, to make sure it's all yours:
If you lean to the left you go left, if you close your eyes you stay where you are.

Which decision are you delaying, canceling, revoking?

But if the umpire admits his mistake, doesn't the game need to be replayed?

Moon-face, cried to sleep and screamed awake,

The night bright and shining through the snow-filled garden under the window.

I can imagine it being like this:

Awake in the middle of the night, snow on the branches, the sky full of stars.

Ghalib, they take you for someone who has some knowledge about something,

Because you have written that you are already happy when your longing is met with an impatient gesture.

## Victory

Once we have it, what do we do?
    Another victory like that and we—what will we be?—we will
be lost.

If you want to take over my job, you will have to work harder
    To convince me that I have succeeded at everything possible
that will lead to my being lost.

My clothes on the beach, everyone gets their own back, but not
me.
    I should have known I would lose them if I left them lying there.

Lying in the sea when the beach is empty,
    An unexpectedly large wave washing over me like another victory.

## Showing What I Am Hoping For

When I dream I am flying, the air is like water.
  I don't need to do much to stay up in the air, if I wave my right
hand I go to the left.

When I say goodbye to all of you,
  I don't want to have left behind too much that I hoped would
make me rich.

Because I never asked for it,
  Someone stops what he is doing and decides if he can help me
if I ask him to.

All the things I hope I won't have to do.
  I hope I won't even have to explain. Have you ever heard anyone
hope for so much?

A list of everything I could have, then I could easily cross off
what I have,
  And if I lose everything later, I will have somewhere to start.

Ghalib is working on a list of everything I hope for,
  But that has a different purpose.

## Just Say Yes, I Promise I Will Do All the Work

The one I search for all evening, with a lamp in my hand,
    Pressed into my hand like a bunch of wildflowers.

The one I want to have pick me up,
    Though I don't arrive anyway, which of us has flowers?

You had told me it would be a surprise,
    What did I think it would be, green birds among red flowers?

What do you want to object to, the flowers in my hand?
    Can I lay them down without one of the flowers being further
away than the others?

# What an Idiotic Idea, My Being the First to Start Work if I Start in the Dark

If something is almost enough, will you add something?
    Can you top up my glass to the rim, just to be on the safe side?

The plan was for somebody else to do my job and I wouldn't even know who.
    I would walk around somewhere I could find it easily and take it home with me.

If you ask me what I want, I hope I sound boastful.
    It's another evening I would like to spend somewhere boastful people talk to each other.

What an idiotic wish, wanting someone to read what I have written, even if I still have two more.
    I wanted to be able to say I only write because they are waiting for a poem this evening.

So much has to come together at once when someone wants to write a poem.
    Can you imagine what it takes to write another one?

I am good at misunderstanding what is being said,
    And then turning what I have heard into something I should be able to answer questions about.

Ghalib is there, pacing and thinking up a poem to read tonight.
    You cannot imagine him ever having done anything else.

## Ghalib Thought of This

The king sends me letters and in each letter he has underlined words.
  Will I please turn them into poems?

A uprising has broken out,
  And the king has promised to lead it, that is why he has no time left for anything else.

I leave the letters untouched for as long as possible.
  When he sends someone to remind me, I do it as quickly as possible.

It doesn't take long, because they are not my poems.
  If the king wants them to say something else, he can change anything he likes.

The king can hardly move anymore.
  The mail is no longer delivered, but there is someone who has thought of a solution.

Ghalib writes a letter explaining a poem.
  Anyone who reads it only gets more confused and passes the letter on to someone else as quickly as possible.

## On a Horse

I want to learn how to ride but there aren't any horses left.
    If I like I can come back at night and ride a horse in the dark.

The horse steps to the side when I try to climb onto it.
    Does it get scared when it's dark and someone suddenly wants
to learn how to ride?

Each of the horse's steps toward heaven
    Takes the man on the horse as far as he can see in the dark.

Muhammad returns from the highest heaven to the highest heaven
but one,
    Moses asks what news God has instructed him to bring down
with him.

Moses says that God is asking too much, go back and ask if it
could be less.
    If you would rather not ask yourself, perhaps Abraham can do
it for you.

Does someone in a lower heaven notice when someone in the
heaven above them walks over the floor,
    Staying as quiet as possible themselves as a result?

Imagine what it is like for someone to ride from heaven to heaven
on a horse,
    On the stairs, in the middle of the night, in the dark.

When Ghalib was a child he was sure he had never felt love.
    How was he supposed to find out what it was like?

## Desire

I wished my only problem was your not wanting to see how I desire you.

It's not a pretty sight, if I had a choice I would look away too.

Every time I stop I lay down my desire, my eyes too tired to see who is standing before me.

Is that what I call a desire? I only want to learn how to do something.

Get changed, I mean, get undressed.

You are the only one who is left, everything around you is empty, not because you desire someone.

Turn around, turn around, turn around.

I see you—if I say I see you, you can come out.

Ghalib complains that you are not doing your job.

What he thought was his due, if others get it why not him?

I have heard that less desire helps, but wouldn't more desire save me from this,

Like someone saving the life of someone he doesn't want to talk to?

No one knows what desire is until Ghalib says something about it.

He reads the history of the world and when he is finished, he says what is missing.

# Desire

The naked king in a slow chariot, on the streets of his new capital.
   The horses have hardly slept, he woke them long before dawn.

Who would want to live here apart from the masons and painters
who still have work to finish?
   They wake them up in the middle of the night and give them
five minutes to get dressed.

If the king says he has conquered twenty cities, there must be
something he has brought back home with him.
   He sees an empty field and immediately begins to build a new
capital.

Night and the horses know who I am and the empty plain knows
who I am.
   Ghalib, if you know what's good for you, you will write a letter
to the little queen with the two ministers,

The one women long for more when they know they don't have
much time left,
   And the one who speaks to women in the street when it has
grown dark.

Someone gets beaten to death in the street for almost nothing, his
shirt perhaps.
   The reason they don't touch Ghalib? Because he once wrote a
letter to their queen.

## The News of the Day

If I am careful enough I can try to write on anything, I can even write in the air.

Fine by me, is it something I want to try, if it's a matter of giving without wanting to receive anything in return?

A hand filled with sugar for the birds that are willing to eat out of someone's hand.

There is so much air, but if I want to do something with it I can have it all.

I keep on wanting to look to see whether something I cannot begin or end has already begun.

Do I think that something has changed somewhere faraway, what was the news today?

Am I not proud of having to start every day at the beginning,

As it would take me more than a day to work out where I had left off?

What I am trying to do when I start by writing down everything I know about something,

Is that like writing down what does not yet exist without thinking that it is better than it is?

I can't keep what has existed from the beginning as mine, I don't have the time to go back and forth.

It frightens me if less and less is left, even if none of what existed then was mine.

Is there anything that was once mine, that I can pick up, long after
I said my goodbyes?
   If you remember that you didn't buy it and weren't given it, you
won't want to keep it anyway, will you?

Say something like the way the world was made,
   Not like it is, but as if I can go back or listen.

If I desire something it is also there, in the same way that it can
also no longer be there,
   Except when I long for something that has never been made.

Someone asked me what I was good at—ah, they can always try.
   I am gradually discovering that what I write is like something
that used to be something else.

## Exactly That Much

Waving a beggar aside, but still giving him what he's asking for
  If he stays standing in front of me, exactly that much!

I give him money to buy drink, but five minutes later he's standing
in front of me again,
  Asking, before he recognizes me, for exactly that much!

When he speaks to me, I smell that he doesn't smell of drink,
  And no, he's not getting money from me a second time, exactly
that much!

Making myself come, when I am far away from where I want to
sleep,
  Not asking someone, for exactly that much!

Can I remember something I used to really want and don't
anymore?
  If I'm honest I can't think of anything, I still want it, exactly
that much.

Do I think it would help if I didn't want something anymore, it
wasn't that much?
  It's not that it would help to want less and less, it isn't that
much.

You can cut the heart out of my body if you say that is what I
owe you, exactly that much.
  I didn't make that up, I got it from an old Jew, he said I could
do what I like with it, exactly that much.

## It Would Be a Good Joke
## If Ghalib Were the Only Poet

Ghalib hasn't prayed a day in his life, should he start now he can
no longer speak,
   Gesturing a number of times a day as if he would like to say a
prayer?

That is Ghalib telling his friends they shouldn't stop
   Giving him their poems to improve.

Not because he loves poetry, don't be ridiculous,
   But like a woman defending the man she has been married to
her whole life.

I know a secret I want to tell all my friends,
   I can tell from the poems you have sent me that they're not the
first you have ever written, and you're not asking for anything
either.

Give me a poem and the next day I'll give it back improved, unless
I have lost it.
   If my hands can't hold anything anymore, you mustn't give me
anything anymore.

When I am no longer here, they can give it to you, the bloodied
flag I gave my life for.
   There are many good poets but I would rather wait outside
until it's Ghalib's turn.

## Another of Ghalib's Jokes

I go from door to door like a dog or a cat because otherwise I have nothing to eat.
　　Sometimes they give me something because they have heard I write poems.

It's a joke the way one tries to be more generous than the other.
　　Each time a door opens, I look as if I am longing for something, I can see it in their faces.

You're right, I write as if I am translating from another language
　　And doing my best to stick as closely as possible to the parts I have understood.

I wished that someone could explain to me what a poem is to someone who is not human,
　　Then I might be better able to explain what a poem is.

Weren't you going to cut off someone's head today? someone asks.
　　Today? Whose head would that be?

While I explain to you where I am, as if explaining a joke before telling it,
　　You come up behind me—please don't scare me like that.

I can't joke about everything—not that I always manage to come up with a joke—
　　And then say something as if I mean it and it will be ruined if someone doubts it for even a second.

Don't tell Ghalib that he is ironic, because he doesn't want to be,
　　Except when his breath has been taken away—yes, then he
wants to be ironic.

Again Ghalib says something that is just a little too wise, instead
of something like one prime number after the other,
　　So that those who hear it are almost certain that thought has
gone into what is being said, can't he do better?

## Like This

If you ask me what something is like, as if I know everything, can
I say, like this?
    I would like that, being able to say it is not how you thought, it
is like this.

How long can I say, no, that is not how I want to remember it?
    How long can I say, I already know something I don't want to
remember?

I can come to you and stay part of the night. You can say whether
it's going to be the first or last part.
    Until you say it is not like you thought it would be, like this.

A house for you in which I can also spend the night, I enter earlier.
    Shall I wait until you arrive and sleep on the floor in my
clothes until then?

If you can choose what you want to remember it's like writing
down what you want to remember, like this.
    Can you search for what you want to remember afterwards, like
this?

How long will I be a rich man and able to order food when I sit
down at a table in a restaurant?
    Why do I always exaggerate so much?

Why do I act like my heart has stopped for a moment when I
want to say something?
    Next thing they will hit me, as hard as they can on the heart,
because I have lain down on the floor.

# Desire

What if I send you ahead and follow behind, every evening you
will see me arriving out of the darkness.
   Can you flick a light on and off just after you get there?

I think about what you are doing, that makes me resemble you
and the one you are doing it for at the same time.
   What can I do for you in return, to close all accounts?

If I saw you, I would long for you too much to be able to tell you
what to do.
   It is such a strange sight, as if you think you have made time stop.

You start there and I start here, and we have something that goes
from you to me and back again while we run towards each other.
   That is for calculating what?

I say that desire has me walking in the dark,
   But you say that there is someone inside of me who decides
where to go.

Ghalib makes a long journey to see how the wind and waves no
longer need to do anything.
   An iron machine pushes an iron ship over the sea.

## Here I Am

I am sitting on the side of the road, there is nothing else here.
    Everyone can get past, they don't need to ask me to move out
of the way.

It was already too late for someone to approach, down an empty
road.
    Flowers left and right, as if I have suddenly remembered having
seen them and was sure at the same time that I was mistaken.

I turn off the light and think for a moment that I can see another
light.
    But as my eyes adjust to the dark I realize it isn't there.

Nobody comes past except perhaps a boy and his animals.
    Ghalib likes to hear about those who can do what he cannot,
he can work with the difference.

## Later

Where you slept, there is nothing left to see,
    As if you slept in your clothes.

Later in the day, when the sun is high, it is too bright to look,
    And you rest, somewhere in the shade, far from where you will
sleep tonight.

The night is almost over, the musicians are still playing,
    Except the one who wakes up when I look at him, the moon
just over his head.

I keep arriving at places where the best is already over.
    If you can still remember it, I ask you how it came to be over,
maybe that will be of some use to me.

If I come I will come later, maybe when the thing everyone came
for is over.
    Surely that is almost an invitation.

I give you a letter and ask you to give it back to me the next day.
    It is an invitation, I was glad to receive it, it must be almost as
good as an admission ticket.

Those clothes suit you, who will you give them to after you have
really worn them for the first time?
    Not just to try them on or to show your new things.

Made up and in my most beautiful clothes, do you have
something for me to wash my face with?
    Or shall I use the clothes I won't wear again anyway?

See it passing by like a river that flows back and forth through the garden.

That is enough for me, even if I have to top up the water every evening.

That is what I wanted, isn't it? Promises for later everywhere I look.

Being able to come in through the front door, isn't that what I wanted?

I write it down to be on the safe side,

Because I wouldn't dare ask what it was again if I forgot it.

I mustn't say that later there won't be anyone willing to let me in.

And if you say that you will always let me in, I mustn't say that later I will not be able to ask that anymore.

I still have a get-out-of-jail-free card, a letter I have not yet opened.

I can have more of something, or I can have something later.

When the announcer of morning recites poems by the one who remembers everything that can be asked of him,

Even the Messiah who came but would not allow us to begin will begin to dance.

# Skipping

Am I one of those who are rich exactly one day a week?
    At the end of the day I don't even need to return what I have before going to sleep.

I am afraid I will feel indignant if someone asks me
    To write a report on what I have done that day.

I almost drop something and begin searching the ground for the shards,
    But I am still holding it in my hands.

I have been doing this for so long that I can sometimes skip part of it,
    But I wish everyone the best at the end of each sentence I say.

I am willing to pay to see me doing it,
    But when it is over I don't care how it has ended.

I skip something, you and I know what.
    We can always do it again later.

I am just someone who tries to do everything that's not the last thing as quickly as possible,
    Nothing behind me but the glory of the night.

This is what I will never see again, but it is not important to me.
    I have only been here a few days, why would I keep looking at it for a long time the last time I see it?

If I want to celebrate something I can rent the biggest room I can find,
    And keep going as long as possible, like celebrating having come first or last.

After midnight: peaches and apricots,
    If I know what I am too late for and what I can skip.

# Bed, Tree, Heart

You take my heart out of my body and lay it in water until the blood has drained out of it.
      You throw it away and a dog thinks I threw it and brings it back to me.

My bed is not deep, when I hear my name called I leap to attention next to it.
      Is that the best I have to offer?

I climbed into a tree to see where you were,
      When I heard that it was you and you didn't know how to get back.

I bump into a tree that hardly moves,
      Unless you count everything moving, like a dog in a train.

Does the bride only start to run after she has been paid for,
      Or does the bridegroom start to run when it gets dark, to meet the bride?

The evening I saw you running ahead of me,
      As if you were getting more out of each step than you were putting into it, and I could see your face from the side because you were looking around.

I move my mouth as if dreaming of eating, it doesn't taste good and there's so little of it too.
      I only asked the price, no reason to get angry at me.

I am not there, do not search for me from all the directions I look in.
      Pay to be what? With all of the heart that can be used to pay.

157

## Letters

I read letters I have been waiting for.
    I know how it ends and I would like to change it because there
are not enough letters.

I would like to stop myself on the stairs,
    When I left a day earlier to get one more letter.

I overtip the paperboy.
    Do I want two newspapers because I am afraid he might suddenly
stop coming?

Or did I mean the mailman, not the paperboy,
    But how can the mailman give me twice as much?

What I get when I don't need to look:
    I become like the paperboy and the mailman who have long
since stopped coming because they have different jobs now.

Those who deliver the mail today can pick out two or three letters
for themselves.
    A mailman can be anything he likes, rather mailman than lawyer.

This afternoon I spoke to a lawyer, rather mailman than lawyer.
    I turn on all the lights because you don't want to come into a
dark house where somebody is home.

This is all in letters to read if I want to go back home today,
which isn't possible because I am far from home.
    Why so many letters, wasn't one enough?

My exact address only confuses the mailman.
    Write: Ghalib, Delhi, and your letters will arrive, I promise.

## Letters

Ghalib announces in the newspaper that he is too weak to answer letters.

If someone comes to visit, he asks him to answer a letter for him.

Don't complain that the letter is not in his handwriting.

He can still say things, but he can no longer listen, that's something he was never any good at.

If someone comes to visit he asks him to write down what he wants to say,

Like in a letter, but he gets an answer right away.

One day I thought I knew exactly what I needed to do to be allowed to enter paradise.

I went to visit Ghalib and wrote a long letter to convince him to do just the same.

Every time I remember that I am so ashamed I cry out for help.

Ghalib said that he was almost dead and that he had done everything wrong his whole life.

When he is dead, his friends can tie a rope around his ankles

And drag him behind them as they stroll through the streets of the city.

The way I think about Ghalib does not have anything to do with whether or not he keeps to the rules

Thought up by someone else, perhaps his best friend.

A friend comes to tell me how I could have done something better, someone should console me.

I have always known that he could get drunk, but not so drunk
that he no longer knows what he is doing,
    And hopes to get rich by striking it lucky for once, something
he doesn't manage.
        He always loses, but I want to do what he says when it
comes to beginnings and ends.

Ghalib is happy with letters that only contain insults,
    At least he doesn't have to answer them before he is dead,
        From now on he only answers letters of love.

## Can You Do That for Me?

I give up traveling because I am afraid of forgetting where I have
already been,
  As if where I have been needs those memories.

Was it you who was scarcely able to set one foot in front of the
other or was it me?
  How do I clean the house afterwards, as if I've never been there,
not a single day?

If I were afraid that you would no longer be able to come
somewhere I would furnish a room
  The way I remember it, but I wouldn't do it for myself.

I know what I have to do something for to be allowed to take it
home with me,
  Though I didn't pay attention when it was discussed.

If I can't ask for something, I can get someone else to do it for
me, by saying,
  Idiot, how can you want to sleep the one night I am with you?

What I can offer someone who works for me: choosing something
I don't have.
  He says, you are so deep in me I breathe for you.

If I am out on the street in the daytime, it is all right to remind
me of something.
  In my home or when it's dark outside, I should be left in peace.

My house is big enough to use one room just as a desert,
  Walking long distances without anyone telling me where to go.

A room like a sea with a bed in it that is like a sea,
  And a room that is only for the light of early morning.

If I get one wish I won't ask for something that can be taken from
me,
  I will ask for everyone to have too much of everything.

If I can ask for something for just me afterwards,
  I will ask for a house with more rooms than I can remember.

## This Evening's Question

Would I prefer to sit with you on the edge of the sea,
    Or on the bank of a river with, on the opposite bank, a plain
or a dense forest?

I wait while it grows dark,
    As in a big ship that I have just bought with a captain who is
ready to take over at any moment.

I touch what you give me, then you can take it back
    Or leave it with me.

Love with time as its friend,
    Have you saved a question for this evening, one you want me to
ask?

# Giving Up

I am not good at giving, but I think I am not bad at giving up.
    If you would like to have it so much, just take it.

Giving up something by going away, in how many places can I be
at once?
    After all, possession is nine tenths of the law.

I have heard that the law is not in heaven,
    So I won't need to play my lawyer there.

What is as if I can still call it back?
    It doesn't come back, but it listens.

Then it finally comes, I know that it is coming,
    But each time it takes long enough to give up on it.

Is there anything I can do to be able to hold what I want in my
hands,
    Even if I have to give it back immediately afterwards?

Surprised by heavy rain, sheltering in the shade of a tree,
    Those who arrive too late start to take off their wet clothes.

I am willing to give up something I'm good at, like writing
lawyerly letters.
    I will ask you to take them for me and give them to me the next
day.

I will not say, I have already given up so much,
    Why must I give that up too?

## Asking for Something

Why don't I ask for something big when I notice that I am being listened to.
    The one who hears my requests and carries them out is hiding.

If something is desired it also exists, in the way that it can also no longer exist,
    Except when I desire something that has never been made.

There is absolutely nothing I want except to sit in the shadow of the one I long for,
    Moving with her when she moves, to stay in her shadow.

If I could make something else yet, I would make someone from clay and put so much water in the clay that it stays soft,
    Or someone from water if I could really make something.

Like a boy making something from paper that looks almost nothing like what he wants,
    But that way he doesn't need to ask for it out loud, and he hopes that it can be larger than he can say.

If I got something without asking for it and no longer have it, I can ask for it.
    If I can say that I want something if I don't get it anyway, I seem to have forgotten how big the world is.

I want to ask you something as if you have already said, why don't you do it yourself? and I have walked away in silence.
    One day you tell me when what I asked for that day was still possible.

You give something away but ask if you can see it again whenever you ask.

You would come to me and I would let you see it.

If it is no longer possible to say of anything that it is worth something else,

I think that I can no longer say no if someone gives me something I once asked for, because it would be like taking something from someone who hardly has anything.

Making a house from paper because I want to ask you something I can only ask in a house.

Letting the wind blow the house apart and letting you get used to not having a house.

From the distance you can look at the only wall still standing.

Then suddenly making a new house for you, without your having asked for it.

So large and beautiful that you would hardly notice if I wanted to sleep there too.

But it remains your house, and if I stay the night, I get up early and stay away until it has grown dark.

You can write something on the door if you want me to wait by the door until you have finished something.

What a plan, I must know a lot about what I do to come up with something like that.

When I am standing at the door, do you know who is standing
there next to me? The one who can never say no to anything,

Like the moon the way I once drew it, a circle in the dark, so as
not to ask for it anymore.

You ask for as much as I am willing to give, but I have already
given all of that away,

But Ghalib, you know exactly what it's like to ask for something
that was given away long ago?

## Any More Questions?

Each time I get fired they ask me later
    To come back for a few days.

I shouldn't lose heart if I hear them say
    Things haven't worked out the way they hoped when they saw
me for the first time.

I'm giving up buying new clothes because I have enough clothes I
have never worn,
    But they're not new, they were bought for this very purpose
long ago.

Just say you don't want to hear that I have been fired again,
    Because that's something different from ransoming me, when
will I start to behave?

That's what you get for asking me too often what I want to be.
    A day will come when you will no longer ask me that, you will
have asked it so often.

# Bird

The bird in the cage speaks with the bird from the garden,
    Where lightning struck yesterday, it saw it through the window.

The bird in the cage says that the bird from the garden
    Doesn't need to be afraid to say what it was like in the garden.

On an evening when the window is open, lightning strikes the
cage and the cage burns to ash in an instant.
    The bird from the garden doesn't need to be afraid to say what
it was like in the garden at that moment.

I write on my forehead for when I can no longer speak,
    Glad I learned mirror writing when I was a child.

I am happy to be allowed to stand here before you,
    Because, because,
        Because this is my job.

# The Author

Nachoem M. Wijnberg, who was born in Amsterdam in 1961, has published fifteen collections of poetry and is widely seen as one of the leading Dutch poets of his generation. His first collection, *De simulatie van de schepping* ("The Simulation of Creation," 1989), was shortlisted for the prize for best poetic debut, and since then he has won a series of other awards in both Belgium and the Netherlands, including the highly prestigious 2009 VSB Prize for the best book of poetry published in the Netherlands for *Het leven van* ("The Life Of") and the Gedichtendagprijs 2010 for *Divan van Ghalib* ("Divan of Ghalib"). His most recent collection is *Van groot belang* ("Of Great Importance," 2015), a book of poems that are not just about economics, politics and history, but also present specific policy proposals about taxes, elections, constitutional law and the abolishment of debts.

His poetry has appeared in translation in journals and anthologies in English, French, German, Chinese, Italian and other languages. A book of English translations by David Colmer was published in London by Anvil Press Poetry in 2013 under the title *Advance Payment*. An Italian translation of *Divan van Ghalib* was published by La Camera Verde in 2015.

Wijnberg also writes fiction and published his fifth novel, *Alle collega's dood* ("Death to All Colleagues"), in 2015. He has degrees in law and economics, and a Ph.D. in management science. He is currently a professor at the University of Amsterdam Business School.

# The Translator

David Colmer is an Australian writer and translator who lives in
Amsterdam and is specialized in Dutch-language literature—novels
and children's books as well as poetry. He has won many translation
awards including major Dutch and Australian prizes for his body
of work and the prestigious IMPAC-Dublin Literature Literary
Award and Independent Foreign Fiction Prize, both with novelist
Gerbrand Bakker. In 2014 *Even Now,* his translation of a selection of
the poetry of Hugo Claus, was shortlisted for the PEN Award for
Poetry in Translation.

Colmer began translating Nachoem M. Wijnberg's poetry almost
ten years ago. *Divan of Ghalib* is their second book together.